Pflichtmaterialien Abitur Niedersachsen 2026

Schwerpunktthema Abitur Englisch – Pflichtmaterialien Abitur Niedersachsen 2026

von Martina Baasner, Berlin / Dr. Wiebke Bettina Dietrich, Göttingen / Anne Herlyn, Waldkirch / Prof. Dr. Peter Hohwiller, Landau in der Pfalz / Eva Runge, Hamburg / Lars Schüler, Buxtehude

Verlagsredaktion
Aryane Beaudoin, Dr. Marion Kiffe

Umschlagkonzept
Cornelsen Verlag GmbH

Umschlaggestaltung
orangerie grafikdesign, Berlin

Umschlagfoto
Shutterstock.com/agsandrew

Layoutkonzept
Ungermeyer, grafische Angelegenheiten

Technische Umsetzung
Reemers Publishing Services GmbH

www.cornelsen.de

Die Webseiten Dritter, deren Internetadressen in diesem Lehrwerk angegeben sind, wurden vor Drucklegung sorgfältig geprüft. Der Verlag übernimmt keine Gewähr für die Aktualität und den Inhalt dieser Seiten und solcher, die mit ihnen verlinkt sind.

1. Auflage, 1. Druck 2024

Alle Drucke dieser Auflage sind inhaltlich unverändert und können im Unterricht nebeneinander verwendet werden.

Druck: Livonia Print, Riga

ISBN 978-3-06-036811-2

PEFC zertifiziert
Dieses Produkt stammt aus nachhaltig bewirtschafteten Wäldern und kontrollierten Quellen.
www.pefc.de
PEFC/12-31-006

Contents

Module V A Midsummer Night's Dream

Module VI seven methods of killing kylie jenner

Contents

Info boxes

Abbreviations and symbols

adj	adjective
c.	*circa*, approximately
cf.	compare, refer to
f./ff.	and the following page(s)/line(s)
fml	formal
infml	informal
jdn., jdm.	*jemanden, jemandem*
l., ll.	line, lines
n	noun
p., pp.	page, pages
par	paragraph
pl	plural
sb.	somebody
sl	slang
sth.	something
v	verb

□⊙ cornelsen.de The webcode can be entered at *www.cornelsen.de* to connect
+◁) Code: xxxxx you directly to a website with additional material.

◁) Listening task (audio available)

⊙ Viewing task (video available)

Story of an Hour

Part A
Pre-reading activities

A1 A happy couple

1 You are going to read a short story about a couple in the American South a few years after the Civil War. Do some research on that historical period. How did people live at the end of the 19th century in the USA? Prepare a short presentation.

2 a **Think:** Make a list of what it takes to make a relationship a happy one.

   b **Pair:** Speaking With a partner, compare your lists and choose five ideas you have in common.

   c **Share:** Speaking Share your five ideas with the class and, all together, discuss which ones stand out.

A cannon from the US Civil War

Part B
While-reading activities

B1 'Story of an Hour' *Kate Chopin*

Read the short story and complete the tasks on pp. 10–12.

Knowing that Mrs. Mallard was afflicted with a heart trouble, great care was taken to break to her as gently as possible the news of her husband's death.

It was her sister Josephine who told her, in broken sentences; veiled
5 hints that revealed in half concealing. Her husband's friend Richards was there, too, near her. It was he who had been in the newspaper office when intelligence of the railroad disaster was received, with Brently Mallard's name leading the list of 'killed.' He had only taken the time to assure himself of its truth by a second telegram, and had hastened
10 to forestall any less careful, less tender friend in bearing the sad message.

She did not hear the story as many women have heard the same, with a paralyzed inability to accept its significance. She wept at once, with sudden, wild abandonment, in her sister's arms. When the storm of grief had spent itself she went away to her room alone. She would
15 have no one follow her.

There stood, facing the open window, a comfortable, roomy armchair. Into this she sank, pressed down by a physical exhaustion that haunted her body and seemed to reach into her soul.

She could see in the open square before her house the tops of trees
20 that were all aquiver with the new spring life. The delicious breath of rain was in the air. In the street below a peddler was crying his wares. The notes of a distant song which some one was singing reached her faintly, and countless sparrows were twittering in the eaves.

There were patches of blue sky showing here and there through the
25 clouds that had met and piled one above the other in the west facing her window.

She sat with her head thrown back upon the cushion of the chair, quite motionless, except when a sob came up into her throat and shook her, as a child who has cried itself to sleep continues to sob in its dreams.
30 She was young, with a fair, calm face, whose lines bespoke repression and even a certain strength. But now there was a dull stare in her eyes, whose gaze was fixed away off yonder on one of those patches of blue sky. It was not a glance of reflection, but rather indicated a suspension of intelligent thought.

1 be afflicted with sth. (fml): suffer from sth.
2 break sth. to sb.: tell sb. of sth.
4 veiled [veɪld]: (here) hidden, disguised
5 reveal: show
5 conceal: hide
7 intelligence (fml): (here) information
10 forestall sth. (fml): keep sth. from happening (usually sth. bad)
13 abandonment: *Hingabe*
20 aquiver [əˈkwɪvə(r)]: shacking, full of life
21 peddler [ˈpedlə(r)]: seller in the street
23 eaves (pl): *Dachvorsprung*
30 bespeak sth. (bespoke - bespoke) (literary): speak of sth.
32 gaze (n): fixed stare
32 yonder [ˈjɒndə(r)]: far away, over there
33 suspension: *Aussetzen*

35   There was something coming to her and she was waiting for it, fearfully. What was it? She did not know; it was too subtle and elusive to name. But she felt it, creeping out of the sky, reaching toward her through the sounds, the scents, the color that filled the air.

    Now her bosom rose and fell tumultuously. She was beginning to
40 recognize this thing that was approaching to possess her, and she was striving to beat it back with her will – as powerless as her two white slender hands would have been. When she abandoned herself a little whispered word escaped her slightly parted lips. She said it over and over under her breath: 'free, free, free!' The vacant stare and the look
45 of terror that had followed it went from her eyes. They stayed keen and bright. Her pulses beat fast, and the coursing blood warmed and relaxed every inch of her body.

    She did not stop to ask if it were or were not a monstrous joy that held her. A clear and exalted perception enabled her to dismiss the
50 suggestion as trivial. She knew that she would weep again when she saw the kind, tender hands folded in death; the face that had never looked save with love upon her, fixed and gray and dead. But she saw beyond that bitter moment a long procession of years to come that would belong to her absolutely. And she opened and spread her arms
55 out to them in welcome.

    There would be no one to live for during those coming years; she would live for herself. There would be no powerful will bending hers in that blind persistence with which men and women believe they have a right to impose a private will upon a fellow-creature. A kind intention
60 or a cruel intention made the act seem no less a crime as she looked upon it in that brief moment of illumination.

    And yet she had loved him – sometimes. Often she had not. What did it matter! What could love, the unsolved mystery, count for in the face of this possession of self-assertion which she suddenly recognized
65 as the strongest impulse of her being!

    'Free! Body and soul free!' she kept whispering.

    Josephine was kneeling before the closed door with her lips to the keyhold, imploring for admission. 'Louise, open the door! I beg; open the door – you will make yourself ill. What are you doing, Louise? For
70 heaven's sake open the door.'

    'Go away. I am not making myself ill.' No; she was drinking in a very elixir of life through that open window.

    Her fancy was running riot along those days ahead of her. Spring days, and summer days, and all sorts of days that would be her own.
75 She breathed a quick prayer that life might be long. It was only yesterday she had thought with a shudder that life might be long.

36 elusive [ɪˈluːsɪv]: hard to define
39 bosom [ˈbʊzəm] (fml, poetic): woman's chest or breast
40 possess sb.: have a strong effect on sb.
41 strive to do sth.: try hard to do sth.
44 vacant [ˈveɪkənt]: empty
46 course (v): flow quickly
49 exalted [ɪgˈzɔːltɪd]: *überschwänglich*
52 save (fml, old): (here) but, except
58 persistence: *Beharrlichkeit*
59 impose sth.: force sth., dictate sth.
61 illumination [ɪˌluːmɪˈneɪʃn]: clarity, understanding
68 implore sb. for sth.: ask/beg sb. for sth.
72 elixir [ɪˈlɪksə(r)]: magical liquid
73 fancy (n): (here) imagination

She arose at length and opened the door to her sister's importunities. There was a feverish triumph in her eyes, and she carried herself unwittingly like a goddess of
80 Victory. She clasped her sister's waist, and together they descended the stairs. Richards stood waiting for them at the bottom.

Some one was opening the front door with a latchkey. It was Brently Mallard who entered, a little travel-
85 stained, composedly carrying his gripsack and umbrella. He had been far from the scene of the accident, and did not even know there had been one. He stood amazed at Josephine's piercing cry; at Richards' quick motion to screen him from the view of his wife.
90 When the doctors came they said she had died of heart disease – of the joy that kills.

From: Story of an Hour and Athénaise, 1894, pp. 7-9

Sculpture of the goddess of victory

78 importunity: *Aufdringlichkeit*
79 unwitting [ʌnˈwɪtɪŋli]: not aware
83 latchkey: key for the outer door of a house
85 gripsack [grɪpsæk]: travelling bag
88 piercing (adj): shrill, intense and high-pitched

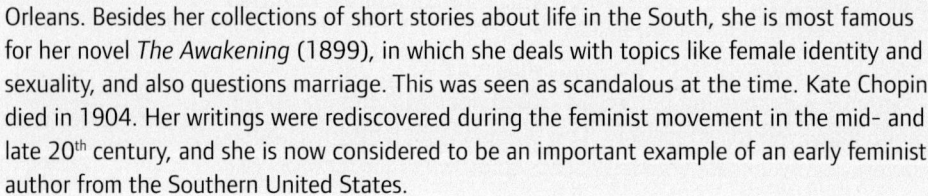

Info **Kate Chopin**

Kate Chopin was born into a wealthy Irish-Creole family in St. Louis in 1850. After her father died in an accident when she was only four, she was raised by her mother and grandmother. Two years after graduation from school, she married Louisiana businessman Oscar Chopin, with whom she had six children. After his business failed in 1879, they moved to a farm in Cloutierville. Following her husband's death, Chopin first kept farming, but eventually returned to St. Louis in 1884. At 39 she began a successful career as a writer of poetry and fiction, working mainly for magazines in St Louis and New Orleans. Besides her collections of short stories about life in the South, she is most famous for her novel *The Awakening* (1899), in which she deals with topics like female identity and sexuality, and also questions marriage. This was seen as scandalous at the time. Kate Chopin died in 1904. Her writings were rediscovered during the feminist movement in the mid- and late 20th century, and she is now considered to be an important example of an early feminist author from the Southern United States.

Comprehension

1 Imagine the story was divided into sections with the subheadings in the table on the next page. In the table, sort the subheadings into the correct order and give line references of the section of the story you would assign it to.

Item	Order	Line(s)
A Thinking about the consequences / Pondering the consequences		
B Sad news (and how to break it to her)		
C The wife's first reaction		
D Newfound strength / Growing into a new role		
E Crushed hopes		
F New perspectives		

2 Fill the timeline below with different emotions Louise Mallard feels in the story.

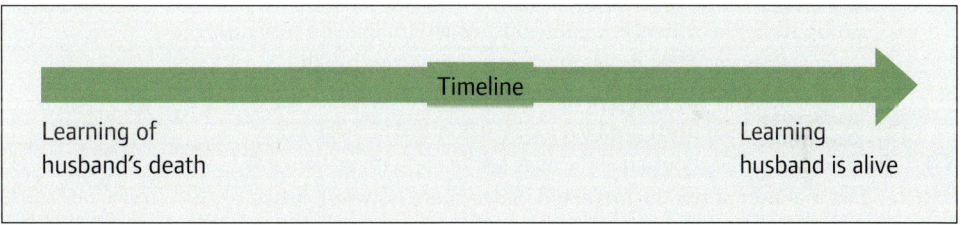

Timeline

Learning of husband's death

Learning husband is alive

Analysis

3 Contrast Louise Mallard and her sister Josephine.

4 Examine how the use of the protagonist's name changes over the course of the story.

5 a Think: In your view, which of the terms below is the most suitable to name the topic of the short story? You may add your own term if you prefer.

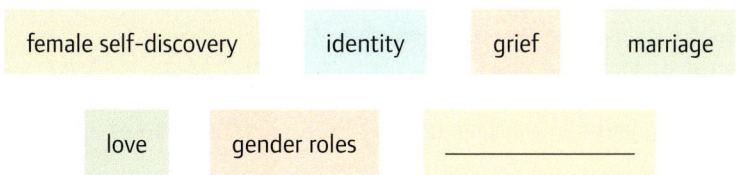

female self-discovery   identity   grief   marriage

love   gender roles   _____

b Pair Speaking: With a partner, compare your results.

c Share Speaking: Explain your choices to the class.

11

6   Analyse how the Mallards' marriage is presented in the story.

7   Examine the author's use of narrative perspective
    (→ Info box, p. 63).

8   Describe the setting of the short story.

9   Irony can be defined as a technique which reveals a distance
    between what appears to be true and what is actually true.
    Discuss if you would call the story ironic.

10   Analyse the use of symbols in the story. Pay particular attention to
    natural phenomena.

11   Discuss the following quote:

> The story is either hopeful or depressing with regard to the changing roles of women.

Beyond the text

12   **a**   Do some research on the historical context of the story,
            especially on the topic of women, i.e. which roles were seen as
            acceptable for women in the late 19th century society.

    b   `Speaking` Present your results to the class.

13   **a**   Hot seat: Work in groups. Prepare to answer the following
            question: Is Louise Mallard a sympathetic young woman or
            rather selfish and cruel?

    b   `Speaking` The first person to play Louise sits in front of the
            group while the others ask questions, which the person playing
            Louise answers. After three questions, the person playing
            Louise chooses the next person to play the role.

    c   `Speaking` Take turns until everyone has played Louise once.

14   The short story 'Story of an Hour' was originally seen as immoral
    and its manuscript was first rejected. Since then, however, it has
    been acclaimed for precisely the reasons it was denounced for
    during Chopin's lifetime. Justify the inclusion of the short story
    into a collection of feminist writing – either in Chopin's lifetime or
    today.

15   `Writing` Rewrite the story or a part of it as a
    first-person narrative for one of the characters.
    Directly or indirectly include three pieces of
    significant information about the character not
    mentioned in Chopin's narrative. Be careful: the
    information should make sense based on what
    you learned in the text.

16   The original first title of the story was 'The
    Dream of an Hour'. Discuss in what way this
    changes your perception of the story and why
    Chopin might have changed it.

Part C
Post-reading activities

C1 A happy marriage?

1 You have been discussing with an American friend how relationships and gender roles have changed in the 21st century. You found an interesting article on this topic in the German magazine *Der Spiegel*. Write a short e-mail to your friend explaining the role of a wife's happiness in a happy marriage. Ask your friend to share their opinion.

Über Eheglück entscheidet vor allem die Frau

Sie sind lange verheiratet und beide Partner zufrieden mit der Ehe? Das klappt am besten, wenn die Ehefrau glücklich mit der Beziehung ist, wie Forscher beobachtet haben. Was der
5 Mann denkt, ist weniger wichtig.

Nach den Ingredienzien für eine glückliche Ehe suchen Forscher schon lange. Was tun, wenn die einst feurige Leidenschaft im Laufe der Jahre immer kleiner wird? Warum schaffen
10 es manche Paare, auch 40 Jahre nach der Hochzeit zufrieden miteinander zu sein – andere jedoch nicht?

Um dies besser zu verstehen, haben Forscher der Rutgers University in New Jersey
15 Daten von fast 400 älteren Paaren ausgewertet, die im Durchschnitt schon 39 Jahre miteinander verheiratet waren. Die überraschende Erkenntnis: Die Zufriedenheit der Frau ist viel wichtiger als die des Mannes, wenn es ums
20 Eheglück geht. Der Mann mag vielleicht gar nicht so positive Gefühle über die Beziehung hegen, solange die Frau glücklich ist, ist alles gut – so in etwa könnte man die Studie zusammenfassen, die im Fachblatt „Journal of
25 Marriage and Family" erschienen ist.

„Ich denke, es liegt daran, dass eine mit der Ehe zufriedene Frau dazu tendiert, viel mehr für ihren Mann zu tun, was sich positiv auf sein Leben auswirkt", sagt Rutgers-Forscherin

Deborah Carr. Männer hingegen würden ge- 30 nerell weniger über eine Beziehung sprechen, sodass ihre Frauen auch weniger über eine mögliche Unzufriedenheit erfahren. Das führe dazu, dass die Unzufriedenheit sich auch seltener vom Mann auf die Frau übertrage. 35

Bei der Befragung der älteren Männer und Frauen wollten die Forscher unter anderem wissen, ob sie sich vom Ehepartner wertgeschätzt fühlen, ob sie sich streiten und ob sie die Gefühle des anderen verstehen. Die 40 Studienteilnehmer wurden auch gebeten, Tagebuch darüber zu führen, wie glücklich sie in den vergangenen 24 Stunden waren, während sie beispielsweise einkauften, fernsahen oder im Haushalt arbeiteten. „Beide 45 Partner waren umso glücklicher und mit dem Leben zufriedener, je besser sie ihre Beziehung einschätzten", sagt Carr.

Die Befragung zeigte auch, dass Frauen unglücklicher wurden, wenn ihr Mann krank 50 wurde. Umgekehrt sei dies nicht der Fall gewesen. „Wir wissen, dass bei einer Erkrankung des Mannes oft die Frau die Pflege übernimmt, was eine stressige Erfahrung sein kann", berichtet Carr. Werde hingegen eine 55 Frau krank, würde meist nicht der Mann, sondern öfter die Tochter die Pflege übernehmen.

From: Der Spiegel Online, *14 September 2014*

The First Feminists

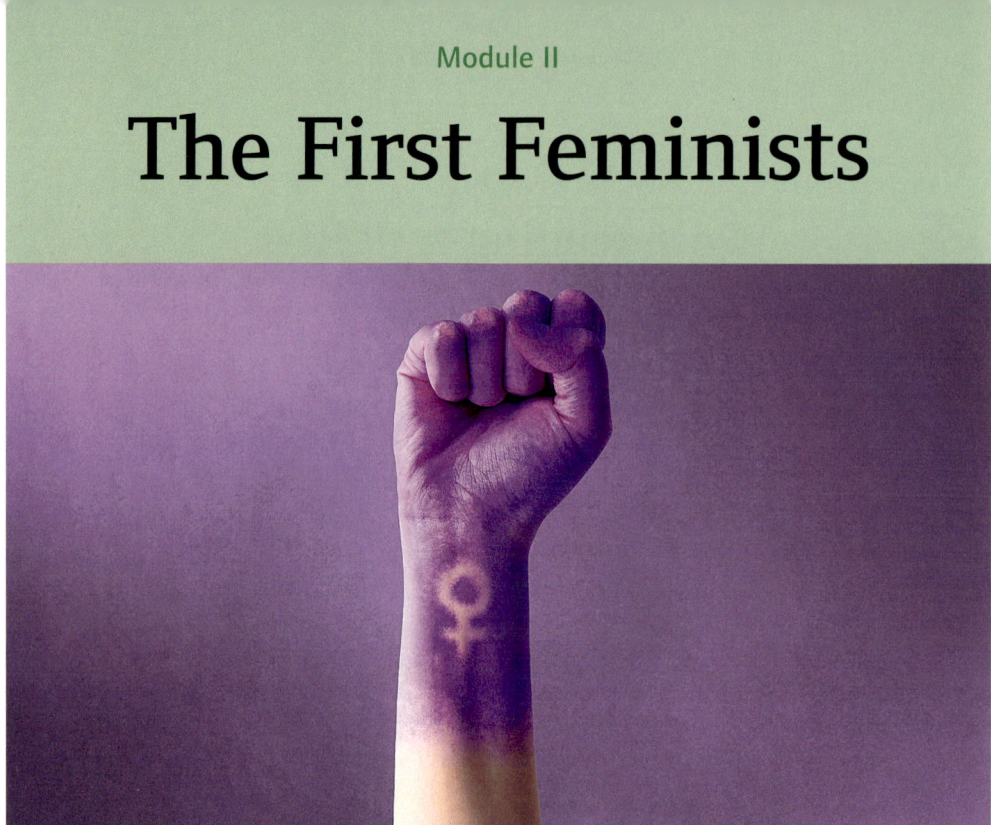

Part A
Pre-reading activities

A1 Feminism and its historical roots

Comprehension

1 Talk to your partner about the symbol above and outline what you
know about it.

2 With your partner, agree on a working definition of *feminism*.

Analysis

3 The symbol above comprises three distinct elements: the purple
colour, the clenched fist, and the symbol of the planet Venus.
Explain what they stand for and how they relate to what the symbol
represents.

Beyond the text

4 **a** Go online and research one of the topics on the next page:

Suffragettism   Riot girl   #MeToo

The Nineteenth Amendment to
the United States Constitution

b `Speaking` Report back to class about your findings and explain
how your topic relates to the waves of feminism outlined in the
info box below.

Info Waves of feminism
Although some researchers consider the idea problematic, it is frequently assumed that
there were several waves of feminism. The first one started in the aftermath of the
French and American revolutions in the late 18th century when women demanded
property rights and the right to vote. In the 1960s, the second wave of feminism
addressed discrimination against women in society and their financial disadvantage.
This is when the fight against the so-called gender pay gap started. A long-standing
critique of feminism (that feminism, i.e. the belief in the political, economic, personal
and social equality of the sexes, largely originated in the West and is predominantly
geared towards white middle-class women) gave rise to the third wave in the 1980s and
1990s and brought attention to racial and social discrimination against Women of
Colour. The fourth wave of feminism started in the 2010s and stands as much against
sexual abuse as it is in favour of female empowerment.

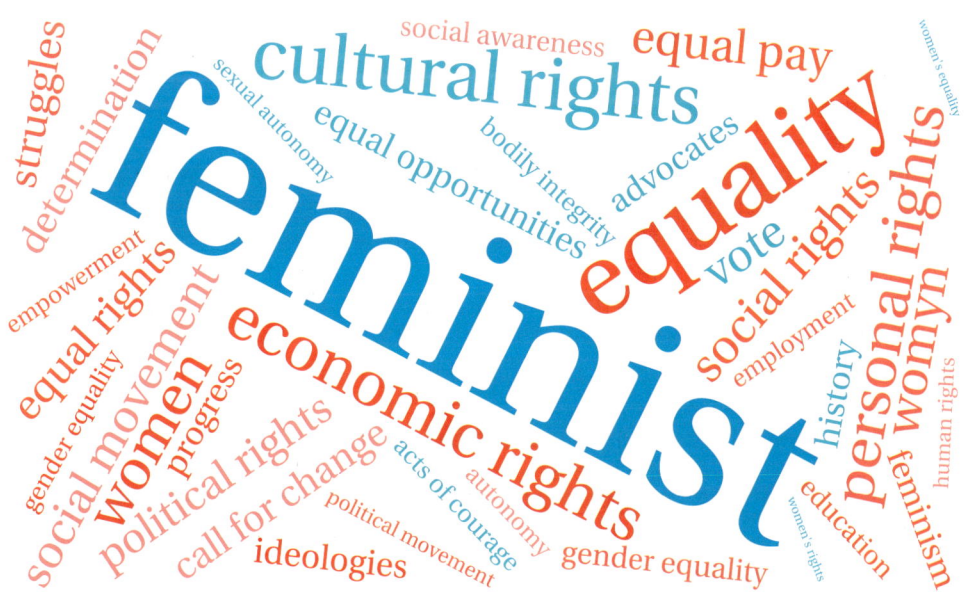

Part B
While-reading activities

B1 'The First Feminists' *Bernadine Evaristo*

1 Work with a partner. Based on the historical insights you gathered in Part A, explain what you expect from a text called 'The First Feminists'.

Reading Read the short story and complete the tasks that follow on p. 20.

we were there when you were just becoming human, unaware that we were carrying the futures of countless billions of souls in our yet to be discovered DNA, unaware we would go on reproducing ever-evolving versions of ourselves, that as the reason for the foetus in every mother's
5 womb, we were the Founding Mothers of the Human Gene Pool

of that we are so proud, we say, when we get together for our annual Founding Mother's Reunion, it dominates the conversation – the human race is here because of us, we boast, only to ourselves, sadly, because nobody can see us, which is a shame, what with the obsession with
10 ancestry DNA these days, we'd love to present ourselves to the world, in the flesh – sashaying down the runway of time in our glad rags, as weird and wonderful role models from pre-history

we were there when you were just becoming human, although we didn't know it back then, we didn't know that humans were beginning
15 to evolve into existence, after the planet's land mass had floated apart and reformed into continents, after the world had gone into a deep freeze during the ice ages, and ice sheets covered the earth and sea, after mountainous icebergs rose up into the cold, blue landscape, sucking the water of the seas into their peaks and freezing them,
20 draining the waterways, which became hollow basins, exposing the continental shelves hidden several miles below in the underground world of oceans, after the ice melted, and the world re-emerged, and the glacial plains of the Sahara thawed out and burst forth with the green and glorious colours of tropical vegetation and impenetrable rainforest,
25 and became ripe with all the fruits and teeming with all the wildlife

we were the first tribes, the first clans, we were the original trail-blazers, after enough of us had developed a maternal instinct towards our offspring, after we stopped walking away from the curious thing that had ejected itself from our bodies, after enough of us learned that
30 the children born out of siblings copulating with each other, and also with their parents, would, in two or three generations, be born with a terrible weakness passed on for generations to come, after we learned to trek and hunt in search of food, and discovered there was more land

3 ever-evolving: become better and better
5 womb [wu:m]: organ of the female body in which babies develop before they are born
8 boast [bəʊst]: say things that show that you are too proud of yourself
9 what with: because of
11 sashay ['sæʃeɪ]: walk in a very confident way
11 glad rags (pl, old-fashioned, infml): clothes that sb. only wears on special occasions
17 ice sheet: layer of ice covering a big area for a long period of time
20 basin: *Becken*
21 continental shelf: edge of a continent that is close to the ocean
25 teem with sth. [ti:m]: be full of sth.
26 trailblazer: pioneer
27 maternal: motherly, like a mother caring for a child
28 offspring (fml, humorous): child
29 eject yourself from sth.: throw yourself out of sth.
30 copulate with sb.: have sex with sb.
32 trek (v): make a long journey on foot

to be found out there in The Great Unknown, after we became intelligent
35 enough to create fire, a powerful, artificial heat, and to work with bone
and stone, after our brains expanded, our arms shortened, our legs
lengthened until finally we became fully upright and slowly made pro-
gress with The Great Migration of Humankind, and eventually arrived
at a location near you – Asia, America, Australasia, the Arctic, Europe,
40 and all over Africa, our homeland, where we all began

it was tough in the early years, we like to remind each other at
our decennial Founding Mother's Reunion, we love indulging in
21st Century social customs like pretending to drink tea and eating
biscuits, playacting at being contemporary humans, when we've actu-
45 ally been around for mega-annums, in one form or another, and how
we laughed at the millennium celebrations just the other day, marking
the transition from the 20th to the 21st Century, as if it was such a big
deal, our descendants really haven't lived at all, unlike us

we who risked extinction over and over again from lack of food or
50 water, from too much heat or too much cold, we who risked extinction
from the relentless battles, especially when our food sources dried up,
or when others came onto the territory we'd claimed as ours, and when
our tribal squabbles led to internecine warfare about who was boss, once
we discovered the power of power, once we realised that having it meant
55 a better chance of survival, and being in control could be intoxicating

we women were all alpha females back in the day, we had to be to
survive, we were so formidable, we'd have it out with anyone who gave
us grief, whether male or female, and believe us when we say, you didn't
mess with the Founding Mothers, the First Ladies of Humanity, because
60 we gave as good as we got, we fought back like the beasts we all were,
we women didn't run screaming when we were confronted with human
foes and expect men to defend us, we often attacked first, it was in us,
we had the primal energy to do combat, we owned our physical strength

the concepts of femininity and masculinity did not exist back in the
65 day, the idea of women behaving in a 'ladylike' fashion took ages to
become normalised, we first humans of Planet Earth shat where we
were, farted and burped with impunity, modesty was a future concept,
we sexed whenever we felt like it, wore no clothes, not even animal
skins or tree barks, not at first, and when we menstruated, we left a
70 trail of blood

we women were equal to men, it was only mothering that tethered
our ambitions, when it became our sole responsibility because men liked
power so much they wanted to keep it all for themselves, but before
then, childrearing was shared equally between all of us, shared between
75 our clan, until the males among us began to pack more muscle density
and grow taller, and began to assume the upper hand, demanding we
stay with the children rather than go hunting for dinner, for our family,
for our clan

42 decennial: after
10 years
42 indulge in sth.: allow
yourself sth. pleasurable
that you know is not
good for you
45 mega-annum ['megə
'ænəm]: one million years
51 relentless: showing no
mercy
53 tribal squabble ['traɪbl
'skwɒbl]: argument
between different tribes
53 internecine warfare
[ˌɪntəˈniːsaɪn 'wɔːfeə(r)]:
fight between members of
the same group
55 intoxicating: (here)
making you feel uncon-
trollable excitement or
happiness
56 alpha female ['ælfə]:
most powerful woman in
a group
57 formidable
[fəˈmɪdəbl]: impressive,
powerful
57 have it out with sb.:
start a fight with sb.
62 foe [fəʊ]: enemy
63 primal: very old,
primitive
67 impunity: fact of not
getting a punishment
69 bark: a tree's outer
layer
71 tether sth. ['teðə(r)]:
tie sth. so it can no longer
move
74 childrearing
['tʃaɪldˈrɪərɪŋ]: process of
raising children

we women fought back, we never stopped fighting back, sometimes
80 we won and men were forced to live in a matriarchal society, other times
men won and we lived in a patriarchy, sometimes neither dominated
and we were egalitarian, which was ideal, we were the first communists,
but it never lasted long because the human desire to dominate each
other prevailed, among us were the first control freaks, dictators, emo-
85 tional manipulators, domestic abusers – and we women survived it all,
we women survived everything pre-civilisation had to throw at us, we
were the ultimate survival experts, we survived on nuts and berries, in
the early days of human life, could go days without water, we slept
rough, lived dangerously, fought wild animals, protected our young
90 luckily for the human race, dinosaurs died out 64 million years before
we emerged, we could not have co-existed on the same planet, our small
communities roaming the plains on two legs would have ended up as
their hors d'oeuvres, eaten live, eaten raw
we were the world's first female leaders, the first feminists, the badass
95 bitches of evolution, whose names will never be remembered because
we had no names, we were anonymous, we will never be recognised as
individuals for our incredible global achievements in ensuring the con-
tinuation of the human race, although we lived long before egos became
part of being human, we do want to be remembered for what we
100 achieved, and we are saddened that we have been reduced to a few
fossils and the imaginations of archaeologists who haven't really got a
clue about our lives, how we lived, the different ways in which we died
– death by disease, before herbs, incantations, health and safety regu-
lations, and medicine, and death by murder, death by tribal warfare,
105 and death by religious sacrifice, once we started to worship deities –
animate and inanimate, seen and unseen, once we became intelligent
enough to want to make sense of the world we lived in and imagined
supreme, all knowing beings who could help us in times of crisis
for the longest time we mated without love, we did not know the
110 meaning of it, although in time we evolved to have feelings for each
other, the modern-day concept of love still amuses us, all the songs sung
about it when companionship and compatibility are more important,
we all agree on that, love is a feeling but if the human race is to survive
then we all have to get along
115 it might seem odd telling you all this now when it was eons ago, but
our lives were important to us and we have been so overlooked, so
misunderstood, and we are the only ones who know it, sometimes at
our Founding Mothers Reunion, after we've had a few gin and tonics
and feel relaxed and comforted by our company, we all fall silent and
120 return to our pre-language selves, to a time when we humans were
hyper-sensitive to each other, when we sensed more than we thought,
when that was enough, when our first sounds were inarticulate grunts,
it took an age for words to come into being and many hundreds of

80 matriarchal
[ˌmeɪtriˈɑːkl]: led/
controlled by women
81 patriarchy [ˈpeɪtriɑːki]:
society led/controlled by
men
82 egalitarian: believing
in equal rights
85 domestic abuser:
person who behaves
violently towards their
partner and/or children
88 sleep rough: sleep
outside on the ground
92 roam sth.: wander
over sth.
93 hors d'oeuvre
[ˌɔː ˈdɜːv]: food eaten
before the main meal
94 badass (adj, infml):
tough
103 incantation: song
that is believed to have
healing powers
105 deity [ˈdeɪəti]: god/
goddess
105 animate: alive
109 mate (v): have sex
(used when referring to
animals)
115 eon [ˈiːɒn] (AE, BR =
aeon): thousands of years
122 inarticulate grunt:
short, low sound that is
impossible to understand

thousands of years for us to create language, to join the words up into
125 sentences, and many more for writing to be invented

imagine a world where there are no words to describe your fellow
human beings, no words for animals, to describe the trees, the forest,
the sea, a child, imagine a world where there was no word for the concept
of family, now we know all the words in all the languages, thousands
130 of them, we have so much knowledge stored in our infinite memory
banks, we are knowledge and because we take the long view, we worry
about what the future holds, we look up into the exploding stars from
a society we never imagined and wonder aloud – what will the human
race become? how will we evolve?

135 we discuss our fears that the human race will annihilate itself before
too long, dehydrate the planet so that it once more dies of thirst, all
plant and animal life withered in the heat, we worry that cannibalism
will return, which is what happens when starving people have to resort
to desperate measures, we worry about the appearance of new diseases
140 that science cannot control, we worry that humans will detonate themselves into inexistence with the last great wars of this civilisation, perhaps there'll be a global Armageddon of megalomaniacal warlords who
are capable of human eradication, of planetary destruction, we worry
that hackers encoded encryptions will one day collapse the cybers-struc-
145 tures without which this society cannot function – the internet virus
that finally closed the world down – the civilisation you are looking for
is no longer available

we worry that everything we fought for might one day no longer be
here, except for us, hovering in the air, a ghostly presence neither seen,
150 heard or felt by modern human beings who have lost their extra sensory
perception, and we will feel so sad that our endeavours over millions
of years might one day come to an end, and then we decide to cheer
ourselves up by wallowing in nostalgia, because we are happiest in the
past, when we were younger, more truly alive and everything was new
155 we remember a time before the internet, before computers, before laws
before cars, aeroplanes, bicycles, penny farthings and horse-drawn
carriages
before factories, before politics, before royalty, before money, before
houses
160 before agriculture, before the idea of work, before marriage, before
enslavement
before the formation of countries, governments, before leisure and
social lives
before cooked food, before sophisticated cognitive reasoning, before
165 science
before pollution, before manufacture, education, dancing, poetry
before we could plan ahead, could think outside of ourselves
before we were able to tell our own stories

135 annihilate sb./sth.:
kill sb./sth.
137 wither [ˈwɪðə(r)]:
constantly become
weaker
140 detonate sth.: set
sth. off (usually a bomb)
142 Armageddon
[ˌɑːməˈgedn]: biblical final
battle between good and
evil which sets the end of
the world
142 megalomaniacal
[ˌmegələˈmeɪniækəl]:
größenwahnsinnig
143 eradication:
destruction
150 extrasensory
perception: knowing
things without using your
senses like hearing or
seeing
151 endeavour (n)
[ɪnˈdevə(r)]: struggle,
hard work
153 wallow in sth.: enjoy
sth., (here) experience
nostalgia as if enjoying it
156 penny farthing: old-
fashioned bicycle with a
very small back wheel
and a very large front
wheel
164 sophisticated
cognitive reasoning:
complex way of thinking

A penny farthing

170 before our songs were sung
we were there
we were there
we were there

From: WePresent, wepresent.wetransfer.com, June 2023

Info Bernadine Evaristo
Born in London in 1959 to an English mother and Nigerian father,
Bernadine Evaristo went to college and university in London,
graduating with a PhD in Creative Writing. She publishes
extensively: her books have been translated into more than
40 languages and the most important accolades have been
awarded to her, including the 2019 Booker Prize (which she shared
with Margaret Atwood) for her novel *Girl, Woman, Other*. She is
Professor of Creative Writing at Brunel University London and President of the Royal
Society of Literature, the second woman and first Person of Colour to ever do so.

Comprehension
2 Describe what the narrators of the text look like. Back up your ideas
  by making references to the text.
3 Describe how, according to the narrators, women gradually lost their
  primordial power.

Analysis
4 Analyse the structure of 'The First Feminists'. Pay particular attention
  to the verb tenses used in the text.
5 Towards the end of 'The First Feminists', several apocalyptic
  scenarios are outlined. With a partner, examine how realistic they are.
  Use the table below to make short notes.

Apocalyptic scenario	How realistic is it? Why?

6 `Writing` The text 'The First Feminists' implies that certain phenomena did not exist for the first feminists because their languages lacked the right expressions. In an argumentative essay, explain whether you agree or disagree with this hypothesis. Use a suitable passage from Evaristo's text as a starting point.

Language help

linguistic gap(s) · signify/denote sth. · stand for / represent/mirror sth. · real-life equivalent · one-to-one correspondence · compatibility/incompatibility between language and reality · word/term/expression/lexical item · object/referent

---

7 Explain to which text genre 'The First Feminists' might belong.

Beyond the text

8 Discuss how Evaristo's story relates to the different waves of feminism as presented in the info box (→ Info box, p. 15) in Part A.

9 a The feminist punk band The Slits released their debut album *Cut* in 1979. Conduct some research on the band and study the iconic cover of *Cut*.

b With your partner, discuss whether or not the album cover might be a suitable accompaniment to Evaristo's text.

Viv Albertine, Ari Up and Tessa Pollitt from the band The Slits in 1979

Part C
Post-reading activities

C1 A feminist icon

Comprehension
1 Describe the poster above.

Analysis
2 Analyse the representation of femininity in the poster.
3 **a** Go online and find out who or what is meant by 'Rosie the Riveter'.
   b Analyse how the poster might have been influenced by 'Rosie the Riveter'.

Beyond the text
4 **a** Go online and select one of the poster's numerous reworkings.
   b Speaking Present one of them, explaining the effects created by reworking the original.

The Yellow Wallpaper

Part A
Pre-reading activities

A1 Zooming in on the text

1 In what kind of surroundings would you expect to see a wallpaper like the one above? Exchange your ideas with a partner.
2 You are going to read Charlotte Perkins Gilman's story 'The Yellow Wallpaper', published in 1892.
   a Read the biographical details on the author in the box on p. 24.

Hand coloured lithographic illustration by Lynd Ward to 'The Yellow Wallpaper', ca. 1935

Info Charlotte Perkins Gilman

Charlotte Perkins Gilman (born 1860 in Connecticut) spent her childhood in poverty after her father had deserted the family. She married the artist Charles Walter Stetson in 1884 and gave birth to their daughter one year later. Suffering from severe postnatal depression, she was treated by Dr Silas Weir Mitchell, who is mentioned in 'The Yellow Wallpaper'. In 1888, Gilman separated from her husband – a rare move in the USA of the 1890s. She went to live with her friend Adeline Knapp and is believed to have been in a serious relationship with her. After some years, in another rare move, she sent her daughter to live with her father. Although publicly frowned upon, Gilman now had the time to focus on her career as a writer, novelist and feminist activist. In 1900, she married her first cousin Houghton Gilman. When she was diagnosed with terminal breast cancer shortly after the death of her second husband, Charlotte Perkins Gilman committed suicide in 1935.

b Among the most frequently used content words in the text are 'John', 'pattern', 'nervous' and 'room'. Imagine what 'The Yellow Wallpaper' might be about, drawing on the information from the info box and on your results from task **1**. Compare ideas with your partner.

3 Reading Study the opening paragraphs of the story. (The words 'ancestral hall', 'colonial mansion', and 'hereditary estate' all refer to a huge old house; 'queer' means 'strange' here).

It is very seldom that mere ordinary people like John and myself secure ancestral halls for the summer.

A colonial mansion, a hereditary estate, I would say a haunted house, and reach the height of romantic felicity – but that would be asking too much of fate!

Still I will proudly declare that there is something queer about it.

Else, why should it be let so cheaply? And why have stood so long untenanted?

a Try to identify the genre of the text.
b With a partner, collect other texts or films you know that have a comparable beginning. Why might such a beginning be so popular?

Part B
While-reading activities

B1 'The Yellow Wallpaper' *Charlotte Perkins Gilman*

Reading Read the first part of the short story and complete the tasks on pp. 29–30.

It is very seldom that mere ordinary people like John and myself secure ancestral halls for the summer.

A colonial mansion, a hereditary estate, I would say a haunted house, and reach the height of romantic felicity – but that would be asking too
5 much of fate!

Still I will proudly declare that there is something queer about it.

Else, why should it be let so cheaply? And why have stood so long untenanted?

John laughs at me, of course, but one expects that in marriage.
10 John is practical in the extreme. He has no patience with faith, an intense horror of superstition, and he scoffs openly at any talk of things not to be felt and seen and put down in figures.

John is a physician, and PERHAPS – (I would not say it to a living soul, of course, but this is dead paper and a great relief to my mind) –
15 PERHAPS that is one reason I do not get well faster.

You see, he does not believe I am sick!

And what can one do?

If a physician of high standing, and one's own husband, assures friends and relatives that there is really nothing the matter with one
20 but temporary nervous depression – a slight hysterical tendency – what is one to do?

My brother is also a physician, and also of high standing, and he says the same thing.

So I take phosphates or phosphites – whichever it is, and tonics, and
25 journeys, and air, and exercise, and am absolutely forbidden to 'work' until I am well again.

Personally, I disagree with their ideas.

Personally, I believe that congenial work, with excitement and change, would do me good.
30 But what is one to do?

I did write for a while in spite of them; but it DOES exhaust me a good deal – having to be so sly about it, or else meet with heavy opposition.

I sometimes fancy that in my condition if I had less opposition and
35 more society and stimulus – but John says the very worst thing I can

1 secure sth.: (here) book sth.
2 ancestral hall [æn'sestrəl]: huge house that has belonged to one family for a long time
3 mansion: huge house
3 hereditary estate: huge house that has belonged to one family for a long time
3 haunted: believed to be inhabited by ghosts
4 height: (here) greatest extent, climax
4 felicity: state of being happy
6 queer: (here) unusual
7 let sth: rent sth. out to sb.
8 untenanted: (here) with nobody living in it
11 scoff at sb./sth.: ridicule sb./sth.
12 figure (n): number
18 of high standing: with a good reputation
24 phosphate, phosphite: (here) kind of medicine
24 tonic: medicine that is supposed to make you feel stronger
28 congenial: pleasant
31 in spite of sb.: even though sb. tried to prevent it
32 sly: secret and/or dishonest
34 fancy sth.: imagine sth.
35 stimulus: inspiration

do is to think about my condition, and I confess it always makes me feel bad.

So I will let it alone and talk about the house.

The most beautiful place! It is quite alone, standing well back from 40 the road, quite three miles from the village. It makes me think of English places that you read about, for there are hedges and walls and gates that lock, and lots of separate little houses for the gardeners and people.

There is a DELICIOUS garden! I never saw such a garden – large and 45 shady, full of box-bordered paths, and lined with long grape-covered arbors with seats under them.

There were greenhouses, too, but they are all broken now.

There was some legal trouble, I believe, something about the heirs and co-heirs; anyhow, the place has been empty for years.

50 That spoils my ghostliness, I am afraid; but I don't care – there is something strange about the house – I can feel it.

I even said so to John one moonlight evening, but he said what I felt was a DRAUGHT, and shut the window.

I get unreasonably angry with John sometimes. I'm sure I never used 55 to be so sensitive. I think it is due to this nervous condition.

But John says if I feel so I shall neglect proper self-control; so I take pains to control myself – before him, at least, and that makes me very tired.

I don't like our room a bit. I wanted one downstairs that opened on 60 the piazza and had roses all over the window, and such pretty old-fashioned chintz hangings! but John would not hear of it.

He said there was only one window and not room for two beds, and no near room for him if he took another.

He is very careful and loving, and hardly lets me stir without special 65 direction.

I have a schedule prescription for each hour in the day; he takes all care from me, and so I feel basely ungrateful not to value it more.

He said we came here solely on my account, that I was to have perfect rest and all the air I could get. 'Your exercise depends on your strength, 70 my dear,' said he, 'and your food somewhat on your appetite; but air you can absorb all the time.' So we took the nursery, at the top of the house.

It is a big, airy room, the whole floor nearly, with windows that look all ways, and air and sunshine galore. It was nursery first and then 75 playground and gymnasium, I should judge; for the windows are barred for little children, and there are rings and things in the walls.

The paint and paper look as if a boys' school had used it. It is stripped off – the paper – in great patches all around the head of my bed, about as far as I can reach, and in a great place on the other side of the room 80 low down. I never saw a worse paper in my life.

45 box-bordered path: *mit Buchs gesäumter Weg*
46 arbor: shelter in a garden made by growing climbing plants over a frame
48 heir [eə]: *Erbe/Erbin*
53 draught [drɑːft]: cold air
61 chintz hangings (pl): *large piece of shiny cloth hung next to a window*
67 base (adj): immoral
68 on sb.'s account: because of what sb. wants
71 nursery: room in which young children play
74 galore [gəˈlɔː] (adj, infml): in large quantities
75 gymnasium: *Gymnastikraum*
75 barred: closed with long pieces of metal or wood

One of those sprawling flamboyant patterns committing every artistic sin.

It is dull enough to confuse the eye in following, pronounced enough to constantly irritate, and provoke study, and when you follow the lame, uncertain curves for a little distance they suddenly commit suicide – plunge off at outrageous angles, destroy themselves in unheard-of contradictions.

The color is repellant, almost revolting; a smouldering, unclean yellow, strangely faded by the slow-turning sunlight.

It is a dull yet lurid orange in some places, a sickly sulphur tint in others.

No wonder the children hated it! I should hate it myself if I had to live in this room long.

There comes John, and I must put this away, – he hates to have me write a word.

We have been here two weeks, and I haven't felt like writing before, since that first day.

I am sitting by the window now, up in this atrocious nursery, and there is nothing to hinder my writing as much as I please, save lack of strength.

John is away all day, and even some nights when his cases are serious.

I am glad my case is not serious!

But these nervous troubles are dreadfully depressing.

John does not know how much I really suffer. He knows there is no REASON to suffer, and that satisfies him.

Of course it is only nervousness. It does weigh on me so not to do my duty in any way!

I meant to be such a help to John, such a real rest and comfort, and here I am a comparative burden already!

Nobody would believe what an effort it is to do what little I am able, – to dress and entertain, and order things.

It is fortunate Mary is so good with the baby. Such a dear baby!

And yet I CANNOT be with him, it makes me so nervous.

I suppose John never was nervous in his life. He laughs at me so about this wall-paper!

At first he meant to repaper the room, but afterwards he said that I was letting it get the better of me, and that nothing was worse for a nervous patient than to give way to such fancies.

He said that after the wall-paper was changed it would be the heavy bedstead, and then the barred windows, and then that gate at the head of the stairs, and so on.

'You know the place is doing you good,' he said, 'and really, dear, I don't care to renovate the house just for a three months' rental.'

81 sprawling: spreading in an untidy way
81 flamboyant: brightly coloured
83 pronounced: obvious, easy to see
84 irritate sb.: make sb. aggressive
84 provoke study: make you want to have a closer look
86 plunge off: (here) move in different directions
86 angle: *Winkel*
88 repellant = repellent: causing strong dislike
88 revolting: very unpleasant
88 smoulder: as if burning with hardly any flame
90 lurid: too bright
90 sickly: not looking healthy
90 sulphur: *Schwefel*
90 tint: colour
98 atrocious: (here) terrible
99 save (preposition, old use): except
118 let sth. get the better of sb.: gain superiority over sb.

125 'Then do let us go downstairs,' I said, 'there are such pretty rooms there.'

Then he took me in his arms and called me a blessed little goose, and said he would go down to the cellar if I wished, and have it whitewashed into the bargain.

130 But he is right enough about the beds and windows and things.

It is as airy and comfortable a room as any one need wish, and, of course, I would not be so silly as to make him uncomfortable just for a whim.

I'm really getting quite fond of the big room, all but that horrid
135 paper.

Out of one window I can see the garden, those mysterious deep-shaded arbors, the riotous old-fashioned flowers, and bushes and gnarly trees.

Out of another I get a lovely view of the bay and a little private wharf
140 belonging to the estate. There is a beautiful shaded lane that runs down there from the house. I always fancy I see people walking in these numerous paths and arbors, but John has cautioned me not to give way to fancy in the least. He says that with my imaginative power and habit of story-making a nervous weakness like mine is sure to lead to all
145 manner of excited fancies, and that I ought to use my will and good sense to check the tendency. So I try.

I think sometimes that if I were only well enough to write a little it would relieve the press of ideas and rest me.

But I find I get pretty tired when I try.

150 It is so discouraging not to have any advice and companionship about my work. When I get really well John says we will ask Cousin Henry and Julia down for a long visit; but he says he would as soon put fireworks in my pillow-case as to let me have those
155 stimulating people about now.

I wish I could get well faster.

But I must not think about that. This paper looks to me as if it KNEW what a vicious influence it had!

There is a recurrent spot where the pattern lolls like a broken neck
160 and two bulbous eyes stare at you upside down.

I get positively angry with the impertinence of it and the everlast-ingness. Up and down and sideways they crawl, and those absurd, unblinking eyes are everywhere. There is one place where two breadths didn't match, and the eyes go all up and down the line, one a little higher
165 than the other.

I never saw so much expression in an inanimate thing before, and we all know how much expression they have! I used to lie awake as a child and get more entertainment and terror out of blank walls and plain furniture than most children could find in a toy store.

128 whitewash sth.: cover sth. with a type of white paint
129 into the bargain: on top of that
133 whim: spontaneous wish for sth. that is not really necessary
137 riotous: (here) growing in every direction
137 gnarly: *knorrig*
139 wharf: *Steg*
142 give way to fancy: let imagination take over control
146 check sth.: control sth.
148 press (n): pressure
153 as soon … as …: (here) rather … than …
159 loll: hang
160 bulbous: fat and round in an unpleasant way
161 positively: (here) really
163 breadth: *Tapetenbahn*
166 inanimate: not alive

170 I remember what a kindly wink the knobs of our big old bureau used to have, and there was one chair that always seemed like a strong friend.

I used to feel that if any of the other things looked too fierce I could always hop into that chair and be safe.

175 The furniture in this room is no worse than inharmonious, however, for we had to bring it all from downstairs. I suppose when this was used as a playroom they had to take the nursery things out, and no wonder! I never saw such ravages as the children have made here.

The wall-paper, as I said before, is torn off in spots, and it sticketh
180 closer than a brother – they must have had perseverance as well as hatred.

Then the floor is scratched and gouged and splintered, the plaster itself is dug out here and there, and this great heavy bed, which is all we found in the room, looks as if it had been through the wars.

185 But I don't mind it a bit – only the paper.

There comes John's sister. Such a dear girl as she is, and so careful of me! I must not let her find me writing.

She is a perfect, and enthusiastic housekeeper, and hopes for no better profession. I verily believe she thinks it is the writing which made
190 me sick!

But I can write when she is out, and see her a long way off from these windows.

There is one that commands the road, a lovely, shaded, winding road, and one that just looks off over the country. A lovely country, too, full
195 of great elms and velvet meadows.

This wall-paper has a kind of sub-pattern in a different shade, a particularly irritating one, for you can only see it in certain lights, and not clearly then.

But in the places where it isn't faded, and where the sun is just so, I
200 can see a strange, provoking, formless sort of figure, that seems to sulk about behind that silly and conspicuous front design.

There's sister on the stairs!

170 wink (n): the act of quickly closing and opening the eyes
170 knob: round door handle
170 bureau: desk with drawers
178 ravages (pl, fml): destruction
182 gouge sth. [gaʊdʒ]: make a hole in sth.
182 plaster: *Wandputz*
193 command the road: allow a view of the road
200 sulk about: be angry
201 conspicuous: easy to see

Comprehension

1 Organize the key elements of the story by taking notes on the following prompts:

How long (will they be there)?

Where?

What (are they doing there)?

When?

Why (are they there)?

Analysis

2 Discuss whether your predictions from **A1**, tasks **1** and **2b** were correct.

3 Analyse the setting of the story. Focus on the house, the garden and the narrator's room.

4 It is revealed that the narrator's room used to be a children's room. Explain the implications this might have.

5 Writing Fill in the following chart about John and his wife, the narrator:

	John	Narrator
Similarities		
Differences		

Beyond the text

6 The narrator remembers, 'I used to feel that if any of the other things looked too fierce I could always hop into that chair and be safe' (l. 171 f.). Explain what or who could serve as the narrator's safe place in her room.

7 Talk to a partner about a safe space from your childhood. It could be a physical space or one that you imagined.

8 Speaking In class, have a discussion on the following thesis: 'In the adult word, there are no safe spaces.'

Reading Read the second part of the short story and complete the tasks on pp. 35–36.

Well, the Fourth of July is over! The people are gone and I am tired out. John thought it might do me good to see a little company, so we just
205 had mother and Nellie and the children down for a week.

Of course I didn't do a thing. Jennie sees to everything now.

But it tired me all the same.

John says if I don't pick up faster he shall send me to Weir Mitchell in the fall.

210 But I don't want to go there at all. I had a friend who was in his hands once, and she says he is just like John and my brother, only more so!

Besides, it is such an undertaking to go so far.

I don't feel as if it was worth while to turn my hand over for anything, and I'm getting dreadfully fretful and querulous.

215 I cry at nothing, and cry most of the time.

Of course I don't when John is here, or anybody else, but when I am alone.

And I am alone a good deal just now. John is kept in town very often by serious cases, and Jennie is good and lets me alone when I want
220 her to.

So I walk a little in the garden or down that lovely lane, sit on the porch under the roses, and lie down up here a good deal.

I'm getting really fond of the room in spite of the wall-paper. Perhaps BECAUSE of the wall-paper.

225 It dwells in my mind so!

I lie here on this great immovable bed – it is nailed down, I believe – and follow that pattern about by the hour. It is as good as gymnastics, I assure you. I start, we'll say, at the bottom, down in the corner over there where it has not been touched, and I determine for the thousandth
230 time that I WILL follow that pointless pattern to some sort of a conclusion.

I know a little of the principle of design, and I know this thing was not arranged on any laws of radiation, or alternation, or repetition, or symmetry, or anything else that I ever heard of.

235 It is repeated, of course, by the breadths, but not otherwise.

Looked at in one way each breadth stands alone, the bloated curves and flourishes – a kind of 'debased Romanesque' with delirium tremens – go waddling up and down in isolated columns of fatuity.

But, on the other hand, they connect diagonally, and the sprawling
240 outlines run off in great slanting waves of optic horror, like a lot of wallowing seaweeds in full chase.

The whole thing goes horizontally, too, at least it seems so, and I exhaust myself in trying to distinguish the order of its going in that direction.

Silas Weir Mitchell

208 pick up: get better
208 Weir Mitchell: Dr Silas Weir Mitchell (1829–1914), US physician who invented the rest cure for patients supposedly suffering from nervous diseases. The therapy encouraged patients to stay in bed and avoid work at all costs.
214 fretful: unhappy and uncomfortable
214 querulous: showing that you are annoyed
233 radiation: the arrangement of things uniformly around a central axis
233 alternation: the arrangement of things following one after the other in a repeated pattern
236 bloated: *aufgebläht*
237 flourish (n): exaggerated movement
237 debase sth.: make sth. less in quality
237 delirium tremens: (here) confusion
238 waddle up and down: walk up and down, moving your body from side to side
238 fatuity: silliness
240 slanting: not straight
241 wallow: move to and fro
241 in full chase: at high speed

245 They have used a horizontal breadth for a frieze, and that adds wonderfully to the confusion.

There is one end of the room where it is almost intact, and there, when the cross-lights fade and the low sun shines directly upon it, I can almost fancy radiation after all, – the interminable grotesques seem

250 to form around a common centre and rush off in headlong plunges of equal distraction.

It makes me tired to follow it. I will take a nap, I guess.

I don't know why I should write this.

I don't want to.

255 I don't feel able.

And I know John would think it absurd. But I MUST say what I feel and think in some way – it is such a relief!

But the effort is getting to be greater than the relief.

Half the time now I am awfully lazy, and lie down ever so much.

260 John says I mustn't lose my strength, and has me take cod-liver oil and lots of tonics and things, to say nothing of ale and wine and rare meat.

Dear John! He loves me very dearly, and hates to have me sick. I tried to have a real earnest reasonable talk with him the other day, and tell

265 him how I wish he would let me go and make a visit to Cousin Henry and Julia.

But he said I wasn't able to go, nor able to stand it after I got there; and I did not make out a very good case for myself, for I was crying before I had finished.

270 It is getting to be a great effort for me to think straight. Just this nervous weakness, I suppose.

And dear John gathered me up in his arms, and just carried me upstairs and laid me on the bed, and sat by me and read to me till it tired my head.

275 He said I was his darling and his comfort and all he had, and that I must take care of myself for his sake, and keep well.

He says no one but myself can help me out of it, that I must use my will and self-control and not let any silly fancies run away with me.

There's one comfort, the baby is well and happy, and does not have

280 to occupy this nursery with the horrid wall-paper.

If we had not used it that blessed child would have! What a fortunate escape! Why, I wouldn't have a child of mine, an impressionable little thing, live in such a room for worlds.

I never thought of it before, but it is lucky that John kept me here

285 after all. I can stand it so much easier than a baby, you see.

Of course I never mention it to them any more – I am too wise, – but I keep watch of it all the same.

There are things in that paper that nobody knows but me, or ever will.

245 frieze [friːz]: *Bordüre*
249 grotesque (n): human or animal form used in a particular style of decorative art in which the real image is distorted into ugliness or caricature
250 headlong plunge: sudden movement downwards with the head going first
260 cod-liver oil: *Lebertran*
268 make out a case for sb.: argue in favour of sb.

290 Behind that outside pattern the dim shapes get clearer every day.

It is always the same shape, only very numerous.

And it is like a woman stooping down and creeping about behind that pattern. I don't like it a bit. I wonder – I begin to think – I wish John would take me away from here!

295 It is so hard to talk with John about my case, because he is so wise, and because he loves me so.

But I tried it last night.

It was moonlight. The moon shines in all around, just as the sun does.

I hate to see it sometimes, it creeps so slowly, and always comes in 300 by one window or another.

John was asleep and I hated to waken him, so I kept still and watched the moonlight on that undulating wall-paper till I felt creepy.

The faint figure behind seemed to shake the pattern, just as if she wanted to get out.

305 I got up softly and went to feel and see if the paper DID move, and when I came back John was awake.

'What is it, little girl?' he said. 'Don't go walking about like that – you'll get cold.'

I thought it was a good time to talk, so I told him that I really was 310 not gaining here, and that I wished he would take me away.

'Why darling!' said he, 'our lease will be up in three weeks, and I can't see how to leave before.'

'The repairs are not done at home, and I cannot possibly leave town just now. Of course if you were in any danger I could and would, but 315 you really are better, dear, whether you can see it or not. I am a doctor, dear, and I know. You are gaining flesh and color, your appetite is better. I feel really much easier about you.'

'I don't weigh a bit more,' said I, 'nor as much; and my appetite may be better in the evening, when you are here, but it is worse in the mor- 320 ning when you are away!'

'Bless her little heart!' said he with a big hug, 'she shall be as sick as she pleases! But now let's improve the shining hours by going to sleep, and talk about it in the morning!'

'And you won't go away?' I asked gloomily.

325 'Why, how can I, dear? It is only three weeks more and then we will take a nice little trip of a few days while Jennie is getting the house ready. Really, dear, you are better!'

'Better in body perhaps – ' I began, and stopped short, for he sat up straight and looked at me with such a stern, reproachful look that I could 330 not say another word.

'My darling,' said he, 'I beg of you, for my sake and for our child's sake, as well as for your own, that you will never for one instant let that idea enter your mind! There is nothing so dangerous, so fascinating, to

302 undulating: having the form of waves
302 creepy: (here) unpleasant
311 lease (n): *Miete*
324 gloomy: without much hope

a temperament like yours. It is a false and foolish fancy. Can you not
335 trust me as a physician when I tell you so?'

So of course I said no more on that score, and we went to sleep before
long. He thought I was asleep first, but I wasn't, and lay there for hours
trying to decide whether that front pattern and the back pattern really
did move together or separately.

340 On a pattern like this, by daylight, there is a lack of sequence, a
defiance of law, that is a constant irritant to a normal mind.

The color is hideous enough, and unreliable enough, and infuriating
enough, but the pattern is torturing.

You think you have mastered it, but just as you get well under way
345 in following, it turns a back somersault and there you are. It slaps you
in the face, knocks you down, and tramples upon you. It is like a bad
dream.

The outside pattern is a florid arabesque, reminding one of a fungus.
If you can imagine a toadstool in joints, an interminable string of
350 toadstools, budding and sprouting in endless convolutions – why, that
is something like it.

That is, sometimes!

There is one marked peculiarity about this paper, a thing nobody
seems to notice but myself, and that is that it changes as the light
355 changes.

When the sun shoots in through the east window – I always watch
for that first long, straight ray – it changes so quickly that I never can
quite believe it.

That is why I watch it always.

360 By moonlight – the moon shines in all night when there is a moon – I
wouldn't know it was the same paper.

At night in any kind of light, in twilight, candlelight, lamplight, and
worst of all by moonlight, it becomes bars! The outside pattern I mean,
and the woman behind it is as plain as can be.

365 I didn't realize for a long time what the thing was that showed behind,
that dim sub-pattern, but now I am quite sure it is a woman.

By daylight she is subdued, quiet. I fancy it is the pattern that keeps
her so still. It is so puzzling. It keeps me quiet by the hour.

I lie down ever so much now. John says it is good for me, and to sleep
370 all I can.

Indeed he started the habit by making me lie down for an hour after
each meal.

It is a very bad habit I am convinced, for you see I don't sleep.

And that cultivates deceit, for I don't tell them I'm awake, – O no!

375 The fact is, I am getting a little afraid of John.

He seems very queer sometimes, and even Jennie has an inexplicable
look.

It strikes me occasionally, just as a scientific hypothesis, – that perhaps it is the paper!

336 on that score: on
that topic
340 sequence: (here)
order
341 law: (here) basic
artistic conventions
344 get well under way
in doing sth.: manage to
do sth.
348 florid arabesque:
with a flower pattern
348 fungus: mushroom
350 toadstool: type of
poisonous mushroom
350 sprout: grow
uncontrollably
350 convolution: twist
367 subdued: quiet

380 I have watched John when he did not know I was looking, and come into the room suddenly on the most innocent excuses, and I've caught him several times LOOKING AT THE PAPER! And Jennie too. I caught Jennie with her hand on it once.

She didn't know I was in the room, and when I asked her in a quiet, 385 a very quiet voice, with the most restrained manner possible, what she was doing with the paper – she turned around as if she had been caught stealing, and looked quite angry – asked me why I should frighten her so!

Then she said that the paper stained everything it touched, that she 390 had found yellow smooches on all my clothes and John's, and she wished we would be more careful!

Did not that sound innocent? But I know she was studying that pattern, and I am determined that nobody shall find it out but myself!

389 stain sb./sth.: leave a mark of dirt on sb./sth.
390 smooch (AE): dirty spot

Comprehension

1 In the box below, make a diagram of the constellation of the characters in the story. You can omit Henry and Julia since they are only mentioned once and do not appear in the story.

the narrator

2 In the second part of the story, some changes take place. Make notes on them in the following table:

Aspect	Change
Narrator's condition	
Narrator's attitude to room/wallpaper	
John's view of narrator	
Narrator's attitude to other people	

Analysis

3 Work on the two tasks below to examine the function of the narrator's room.

   a Make a sketch of the layout of the narrator's room, including the windows and the women behind the yellow wallpaper. What strikes you?

   b Explain the symbolic meaning of the elements in the room.

4 In the extract, two conversations between the narrator and John are presented.

   a Analyse the conversations with regard to power relations.

   b Examine how these power relations become visible in the language used.

5 Explain what the following quote might reveal about the narrator herself. Make sure to examine its syntax and the effect this may have.

'And dear John gathered me up in his arms, and just carried me upstairs and laid me on the bed, and sat by me and read to me till it tired my head.' (ll. 270–272).

Beyond the text

6 a Do some research about rest cures and the effects they had on the patients.

   b Speaking Imagine that a psychologist who is sceptical of rest cures talks to John about his wife's condition. Act out their dialogue.

Reading Now read the last part of the short story and complete the tasks on p. 41.

Life is very much more exciting now than it used to be. You see I have
395 something more to expect, to look forward to, to watch. I really do eat better, and am more quiet than I was.

   John is so pleased to see me improve! He laughed a little the other day, and said I seemed to be flourishing in spite of my wall-paper.

   I turned it off with a laugh. I had no intention of telling him it
400 was BECAUSE of the wall-paper – he would make fun of me. He might even want to take me away.

   I don't want to leave now until I have found it out. There is a week more, and I think that will be enough.

   I'm feeling ever so much better! I don't sleep much at night, for it is
405 so interesting to watch developments; but I sleep a good deal in the daytime.

   In the daytime it is tiresome and perplexing.

   There are always new shoots on the fungus, and new shades of yellow all over it. I cannot keep count of them, though I have tried
410 conscientiously.

407 perplexing: confusing
408 shoot (n): *Seitentrieb*
410 conscientious [ˌkɒnʃiˈenʃəs]: careful

It is the strangest yellow, that wall-paper! It makes me think of all the yellow things I ever saw – not beautiful ones like buttercups, but old foul, bad yellow things.

But there is something else about that paper – the smell! I noticed it
415 the moment we came into the room, but with so much air and sun it was not bad. Now we have had a week of fog and rain, and whether the windows are open or not, the smell is here.

It creeps all over the house.

I find it hovering in the dining-room, skulking in the parlor, hiding
420 in the hall, lying in wait for me on the stairs.

It gets into my hair.

Even when I go to ride, if I turn my head suddenly and surprise it – there is that smell!

Such a peculiar odor, too! I have spent hours in trying to analyze it,
425 to find what it smelled like.

It is not bad – at first, and very gentle, but quite the subtlest, most enduring odor I ever met.

In this damp weather it is awful. I wake up in the night and find it hanging over me.

430 It used to disturb me at first. I thought seriously of burning the house – to reach the smell.

But now I am used to it. The only thing I can think of that it is like is the COLOR of the paper! A yellow smell.

There is a very funny mark on this wall, low down, near the mop-
435 board. A streak that runs round the room. It goes behind every piece of furniture, except the bed, a long, straight, even SMOOCH, as if it had been rubbed over and over.

I wonder how it was done and who did it, and what they did it for. Round and round and round – round and round and round – it makes
440 me dizzy!

I really have discovered something at last.

Through watching so much at night, when it changes so, I have finally found out.

The front pattern DOES move – and no wonder! The woman behind
445 shakes it!

Sometimes I think there are a great many women behind, and sometimes only one, and she crawls around fast, and her crawling shakes it all over.

Then in the very bright spots she keeps still, and in the very shady
450 spots she just takes hold of the bars and shakes them hard.

And she is all the time trying to climb through. But nobody could climb through that pattern – it strangles so; I think that is why it has so many heads.

They get through, and then the pattern strangles them off and turns
455 them upsidedown, and makes their eyes white!

412 buttercup: small flower with yellow blossoms
419 skulk: move around secretly
424 odor: smell
434 mopboard: *Sockelleiste*
435 streak (n): long thin line

If those heads were covered or taken off it would not be half so bad.

I think that woman gets out in the daytime!

And I'll tell you why – privately – I've seen her!

I can see her out of every one of my windows!

460   It is the same woman, I know, for she is always creeping, and most women do not creep by daylight.

I see her on that long road under the trees, creeping along, and when a carriage comes she hides under the blackberry vines.

I don't blame her a bit. It must be very humiliating to be caught
465 creeping by daylight!

I always lock the door when I creep by daylight. I can't do it at night, for I know John would suspect something at once.

And John is so queer now, that I don't want to irritate him. I wish he would take another room! Besides, I don't want anybody to get that
470 woman out at night but myself.

I often wonder if I could see her out of all the windows at once.

But, turn as fast as I can, I can only see out of one at one time.

And though I always see her she MAY be able to creep faster than I can turn!

475   I have watched her sometimes away off in the open country, creeping as fast as a cloud shadow in a high wind.

If only that top pattern could be gotten off from the under one! I mean to try it, little by little.

I have found out another funny thing, but I shan't tell it this time!
480 It does not do to trust people too much.

There are only two more days to get this paper off, and I believe John is beginning to notice. I don't like the look in his eyes.

And I heard him ask Jennie a lot of professional questions about me. She had a very good report to give.

485   She said I slept a good deal in the daytime.

John knows I don't sleep very well at night, for all I'm so quiet!

He asked me all sorts of questions, too, and pretended to be very loving and kind.

As if I couldn't see through him!

490   Still, I don't wonder he acts so, sleeping under this paper for three months.

It only interests me, but I feel sure John and Jennie are secretly affected by it.

Hurrah! This is the last day, but it is enough. John is to stay in town
495 over night, and won't be out until this evening.

Jennie wanted to sleep with me – the sly thing! but I told her I should undoubtedly rest better for a night all alone.

That was clever, for really I wasn't alone a bit! As soon as it was moonlight, and that poor thing began to crawl and shake the pattern, I
500 got up and ran to help her.

480 it does not do: it is not good

I pulled and she shook, I shook and she pulled, and before morning we had peeled off yards of that paper.

A strip about as high as my head and half around the room.

And then when the sun came and that awful pattern began to laugh
505 at me, I declared I would finish it to-day!

We go away to-morrow, and they are moving all my furniture down again to leave things as they were before.

Jennie looked at the wall in amazement, but I told her merrily that I did it out of pure spite at the vicious thing.

510 She laughed and said she wouldn't mind doing it herself, but I must not get tired.

How she betrayed herself that time!

But I am here, and no person touches this paper but me – not ALIVE!

She tried to get me out of the room – it was too patent! But I said it
515 was so quiet and empty and clean now that I believed I would lie down again and sleep all I could; and not to wake me even for dinner – I would call when I woke.

So now she is gone, and the servants are gone, and the things are gone, and there is nothing left but that great bedstead nailed down,
520 with the canvas mattress we found on it.

We shall sleep downstairs to-night, and take the boat home to-morrow.

I quite enjoy the room, now it is bare again.

How those children did tear about here!
525 This bedstead is fairly gnawed!

But I must get to work.

I have locked the door and thrown the key down into the front path.

I don't want to go out, and I don't want to have anybody come in, till John comes.

530 I want to astonish him.

I've got a rope up here that even Jennie did not find. If that woman does get out, and tries to get away, I can tie her!

But I forgot I could not reach far without anything to stand on!

This bed will NOT move!
535 I tried to lift and push it until I was lame, and then I got so angry I bit off a little piece at one corner – but it hurt my teeth.

Then I peeled off all the paper I could reach standing on the floor. It sticks horribly and the pattern just enjoys it! All those strangled heads and bulbous eyes and waddling fungus growths just shriek with
540 derision!

I am getting angry enough to do something desperate. To jump out of the window would be admirable exercise, but the bars are too strong even to try.

Besides I wouldn't do it. Of course not. I know well enough that a
545 step like that is improper and might be misconstrued.

509 spite (n): feeling of hatred
514 patent ['pætnt] (adj): obvious
525 gnaw sth.: bite sth.
539 shriek (v): make a high loud sound
540 derision: strong feeling that sb. is stupid
545 misconstrue sth.: misunderstand sth.

I don't like to LOOK out of the windows even – there are so many of those creeping women, and they creep so fast.

I wonder if they all come out of that wall-paper as I did?

But I am securely fastened now by my well-hidden rope – you don't
550 get me out in the road there!

I suppose I shall have to get back behind the pattern when it comes night, and that is hard!

It is so pleasant to be out in this great room and creep around as I please!

555 I don't want to go outside. I won't, even if Jennie asks me to.

For outside you have to creep on the ground, and everything is green instead of yellow.

But here I can creep smoothly on the floor, and my shoulder just fits in that long smooch around the wall, so I cannot lose my way.

560 Why, there's John at the door!

It is no use, young man, you can't open it!

How he does call and pound!

Now he's crying for an axe.

It would be a shame to break down that beautiful door!

565 'John dear!' said I in the gentlest voice, 'the key is down by the front steps, under a plantain leaf!'

That silenced him for a few moments.

Then he said – very quietly indeed, 'Open the door, my darling!'

'I can't,' said I. 'The key is down by the front door under a plantain
570 leaf!'

And then I said it again, several times, very gently and slowly, and said it so often that he had to go and see, and he got it, of course, and came in. He stopped short by the door.

'What is the matter?' he cried. 'For God's sake, what are you doing!'

575 I kept on creeping just the same, but I looked at him over my shoulder.

'I've got out at last,' said I, 'in spite of you and Jane! And I've pulled off most of the paper, so you can't put me back!'

Now why should that man have fainted? But he did, and right across
580 my path by the wall, so that I had to creep over him every time!

From: The New England Magazine, *1892*

562 pound (v): knock

Comprehension

1 Put the events of the last part of the story into the right order:

Item	Your ranking
A John considers using an axe.	
B John believes the narrator's condition is improving.	
C The narrator is surprised that John has passed out.	
D The narrator locks herself in the room.	
E The narrator becomes aware of a certain smell.	
F The narrator finds her life exciting.	

2 Outline in detail how the narrator's mental condition develops in the last part of the story.

Analysis

3 Explain who the woman or women behind the front pattern of the yellow wallpaper might be.

4 Examine how the story's language and style at the beginning differ from the end when the narrator's mental condition is reaching its climax.

5 Analyse the narrative perspective of the story and discuss how it is suited for the story's subject matter (→ Info box, p. 63).

Beyond the text

6 Imagine you had to turn the showdown that takes place in the short story – i.e. the events that start with John's knocking at the door – into a short film.

   a With your partner, discuss how you would go about the following:
- the narrator's outward appearance
- John's outward appearance
- dialogue: pitch, tone, speed
- predominant camera perspective and movement
- soundtrack
- final frame.

   b Devise a film poster for your film and make a sketch of it. Don't forget to add a title and maybe even a subtitle.

Part C
Post-reading activities

C1 A dubious cure?

'The Yellow Wallpaper' bears some resemblance to experiences made by its author herself. Study Yvonne Roth's and Susanne Lenz' outlines of these resemblances below.

Text 1: A cure with side-effects

Sie solle ein möglichst häusliches Leben führen, mehr als zwei Stunden geistige Arbeit am Tag strikt vermeiden und fortan niemals mehr einen Füller, Pinsel oder Bleistift berühren. Diese ärztlichen Anweisungen sollten die damals in erster Ehe verheiratete Charlotte Perkins Stetson vor
5 weiteren schweren Depressionen bewahren. Zu deren Behandlung hatte sie sich nach der Geburt ihrer Tochter 1886 einer „rest cure"-Therapie unterzogen, die das Motiv für [Gilmans] berühmteste Kurzgeschichte, „The Yellow Wallpaper" (1892; „Die gelbe Tapete", 1985), werden sollte. Der Text präsentiert als Effekt einer solchen Therapie nicht die Heilung,
10 sondern – im Gegenteil – den völligen psychischen Zusammenbruch. Wie [Gilman] selbst, sieht sich auch die Protagonistin der Geschichte nicht länger in der Lage, ihren Aufgaben als Mutter und Ehefrau nachzukommen, wird depressiv und muß sich einer von der Therapie vorgeschriebenen völligen Ruhigstellung und strengen Isolation von der Außenwelt
15 unterwerfen. Sie entflieht dieser als unerträglich empfundenen Passivität jedoch, indem sie die Wahnvorstellung entwickelt, daß in dem Muster der Tapete ihres Krankenzimmers eine Frau gefangen sei.

From: Yvonne Roth. 'Gilman, Charlotte [Anna] Perkins',
Metzler Lexikon amerikanischer Autoren, 2000

Text 2: Keeping women down?

In der fragwürdigen neurologischen und psychiatrischen Behandlungsmethode, die auf eine drastische Ausschaltung aller als Störfaktoren betrachteten Momente im Leben der Patienten zielt und die eigentlichen Ursachen der Depression unberücksichtigt läßt, offenbart
5 sich das Unverständnis nicht nur medizinischer und psychologischer Experten, sondern einer ganzen Epoche gegenüber den spezifischen Problemen weiblicher Identität. Die „Weir Mitchell Rest Cure" steht beispielhaft für unzählige Versuche, Frauen in der Durchsetzung ihrer beruflichen bzw. künstlerischen Interessen zu behindern, sie restriktiv
10 an die gewohnten, allgemein sanktionierten Pflichten und Aufgaben zu binden und ihnen den Weg zur Gleichberechtigung zu versperren. Als ebenso exemplarisch erscheint die innere Emigration, mit der sich

sowohl die Autorin als auch ihre fiktive Protagonistin den massiven Zwängen einer um die Erhaltung ihrer Ordnung und Machtstrukturen
15 bemühten Gesellschaft entziehen und in deren Verlauf sie die als „grundlos" gebrandmarkte Depressionen durch eine Kette von Schuldgefühlen und Selbstanklagen unausweichlich zur individuellen Tragödie eskaliert.

From: Susanne Lenz, *'Nachwort', Charlotte Perkins Gilman:*
The Yellow Wallpaper, 1987

1 Mediation After reading the two texts, you decide to write an additional section to the English Wikipedia entry on 'The Yellow Wallpaper' specifying how the story reflects some aspects of its author's life. Write your Wikipedia entry.

C2 Feminist manifesto and/or gothic fiction?

Analysis

2 Based on your reading of the short story and the two texts in **C1** discuss possible societal implications of 'The Yellow Wallpaper' and Gilman's biography.

3 'The Yellow Wallpaper' showcases how societal repression changes how the repressed think and behave. This becomes obvious when the narrator expresses that she is not good enough for her husband. Analyse some of her behavioural patterns within this context.

4 Analyse the representation of men in the story.

5 'The Yellow Wallpaper' does not only have an important feminist background, it also ticks many boxes of spooky gothic fiction. Explain.

Beyond the text

6 In 2020, US-American artist Kehinde Wiley (cf. p. 129) had a show in London titled 'The Yellow Wallpaper'. Do some research on the exhibition and the portraits shown.
  a Explain how the portraits relate to Gilman's story.
  b Explain how they add a new layer to the text.

7 Speaking The yellow wallpaper constraining the woman trapped behind it is a likely metaphor for patriarchal society. What would you say is the wallpaper that restricts your generation? Give a short speech in class.

Weekend

Part A
Pre-reading activities

A1 Complex relationships

1 We humans can be described as 'social animals': we all look for connections to people in our lives, be it friends or family, lovers, team-mates, etc.

   a Think: Write down three things that are most important to you in your relationships with other people.

   b Pair: Speaking Compare ideas with a partner and explain your choices. Which aspects can you agree on, where do you differ?

   c Share: Speaking Share results with the class. Try to name the five most important aspects and rank them.

2 **a** Work with a partner and do some research on the 1960s and 1970s in Britain. One of you focuses on the situation of women, the other one on the feminist movement. Be prepared to present your results.

   b Speaking Present your findings to a partner.

A2 **Lifestyles**

1 Make a list of the advantages of living in the country versus living in a city.

Living in the country	Living in a city

2 Create an illustration of your perfect weekend.

Part B
While-reading activities

B1 'Weekend' *Fay Weldon*

Reading Read the story and complete the tasks on pp. 58–63.

By seven-thirty they were ready to go. Martha had everything packed into the car and the three children appropriately dressed and in the back seat, complete with educational games and wholewheat biscuits. When everything was ready in the car Martin would switch off the television,
5 come downstairs, lock up the house, front and back, and take the wheel.

Weekend! Only two hours' drive down to the cottage on Friday evenings: three hours' drive back on Sunday nights. The pleasures of greenery and guests in between. They reckoned themselves fortunate, how fortunate!

10 On Fridays Martha would get home on the bus at six-twelve and prepare tea and sandwiches for the family; then she would strip four beds and put the sheets and quilt covers in the washing machine for Monday: take the country bedding from the airing basket plus the books and the games, plus the weekend food – acquired at intervals through-
15 out the week, to lessen the load – plus her own folder of work from the office, plus Martin's drawing materials (she was a market researcher in an advertising agency, he a freelance designer) plus hairbrushes, jeans, spare T-shirts, Jolyon's antibiotics (he suffered from sore throats), Jenny's recorder, Jasper's cassette player and so on – ah, the so on! –
20 and would pack them, skilfully and quickly, into the boot. Very little could be left in the cottage during the week. ('An open invitation to burglars': Martin) Then Martha would run round the house tidying and wiping, doing this and that, finding the cat at one neighbour's and delivering it to another, while the others ate their tea; and would usually,
25 proudly, have everything finished by the time they had eaten their fill. Martin would just catch the BBC2 news, while Martha cleared away the tea table, and the children tossed up for the best positions in the car. 'Martha,' said Martin, tonight, 'you ought to get Mrs Hodder to do more. She takes advantage of you.'

30 Mrs Hodder came in twice a week to clean. She was over seventy. She charged two pounds an hour. Martha paid her out of her own wages: well, the running of the house was Martha's concern. If Martha chose to go out to work – as was her perfect right, Martin allowed, even though it wasn't the best thing for the children, but that must be Martha's moral
35 responsibility – Martha must surely pay her domestic stand-in. An evident truth, heard loud and clear and frequent in Martin's mouth and Martha's heart.

03 wholewheat (adj): *Vollkorn*
13 airing basket: warm place in which freshly washed laundry is kept so that it dries completely and smells fresh
22 burglar: person who breaks into your house to steal sth.
25 your fill: (here) as much as you can eat
27 toss up: (here) decide or choose who sits in the best place
35 domestic: related to the home or household
35 stand-in: person who does your job for a short time
36 evident: clear, easy to see

46

'I expect you're right,' said Martha. She did not want to argue. Martin had had a long hard week, and now had to drive. Martha couldn't.
40 Martha's licence had been suspended four months back for drunken driving. Everyone agreed that the suspension was unfair; Martha seldom drank to excess: she was for one thing usually too busy pouring drinks for other people or washing other people's glasses to get much inside herself. But Martin had taken her out to dinner on her birthday,
45 as was his custom, and exhaustion and excitement mixed had made her imprudent, and before she knew where she was, why there she was, in the dock, with a distorted lamp-post to pay for and a new bonnet for the car and six months' suspension.

So now Martin had to drive her car down to the cottage, and he was
50 always tired on Fridays, and hot and sleepy on Sundays, and every rattle and clank and bump in the engine she felt to be somehow her fault.

Martin had a little sports car for London and work: it could nip in and out of the traffic nicely: Martha's was an old estate car, with room for the children, picnic baskets, bedding, food, games, plants, drink,
55 portable television and all the things required by the middle classes for weekends in the country. It lumbered rather than zipped and made Martin angry. He seldom spoke a harsh word, but Martha, after the fashion of wives, could detect his mood from what he did not say rather than what he did, and from the tilt of his head, and the way his crinkly,
60 merry eyes seemed crinklier and merrier still – and of course from the way he addressed Martha's car.

'Come along, you old banger you! Can't you do better than that? You're too old, that's your trouble. Stop complaining. Always complaining, it's only a hill. You're too wide about the hips. You'll never get
65 through there.'

Martha worried about her age, her tendency to complain, and the width of her hips. She took the remarks personally. Was she right to do so? The children noticed nothing: it was just funny lively laughing Daddy being witty about Mummy's car. Mummy, done for drunken
70 driving. Mummy, with the roots of melancholy somewhere deep beneath the bustling, busy, everyday self. Busy: ah so busy!

Martin would only laugh if she said anything about the way he spoke to her car and warn her against paranoia. 'Don't get like your mother, darling.' Martha's mother had, towards the end, thought that people
75 were plotting against her. Martha's mother had led a secluded, suspicious life, and made Martha's childhood a chilly and a lonely time. Life now, by comparison, was wonderful for Martha. People, children, houses, conversations, food, drink, theatres – even, now, a career. Martin standing between her and the hostility of the world – popular,
80 easy, funny Martin, beckoning the rest of the world into earshot.

Ah, she was grateful: little earnest Martha, with her shy ways and her penchant for passing boring exams – how her life had blossomed

40 suspend sth.: prevent something from being used for a time
42 drink to excess: drink too much
46 why (old-fashioned): exclamation used to express surprise
47 dock: part of the court in which the accused has to stand
47 bonnet: metal part over the front of a car
50 rattle, clank (n): short loud sounds made when hard objects hit against each other
51 bump (n): sound of something hitting a hard surface
52 nip (infml): go somewhere fast and only for a short time
53 estate car (BE): car with a lot of space behind the back seats plus a door at the back for large items
56 lumber (v): move slowly and clumsily
56 zip (v, infml): move quickly
62 banger [bæŋə(r)] (BE, infml): old car that is no longer in a good condition
69 witty: humorous
71 bustling: lively and active
75 secluded: quiet and isolated
75 suspicious: (here) full of mistrust
80 beckon sth.: make sth. come closer
82 penchant ['pentʃənt]: special liking

out! Three children too – Jasper, Jenny and Jolyon – all with Martha's broad brow and open looks, and the confidence born of her love and
85 care, and the work she had put into them since the dawning of their days.

Martin drives. Martha, for once, drowses.

The right food, the right words, the right play. Doctors for the tonsils: dentists for the molars. Confiscate guns: censor television: encourage
90 creativity. Paints and paper to hand: books on the shelves: meetings with teachers. Music teachers. Dancing lessons. Parties. Friends to tea. School plays. Open days. Junior orchestra.

Martha is jolted awake. Traffic lights. Martin doesn't like Martha to sleep while he drives.
95 Clothes. Oh, clothes! Can't wear this: must wear that. Dress shops. Piles of clothes in corners: duly washed, but waiting to be ironed, waiting to be put away.

Get the piles off the floor, into the laundry baskets. Martin doesn't like a mess.
100 Creativity arises out of order, not chaos. Five years off work while the children were small: back to work with seniority lost. What, did you think something was for nothing? If you have children, mother, that is your reward. It lies not in the world.

Have you taken enough food? Always hard to judge.
105 Food. Oh, food! Shop in the lunch-hour. Lug it all home. Cook for the freezer on Wednesday evenings while Martin is at his car-maintenance evening class, and isn't there to notice you being unrestful. Martin likes you to sit down in the evenings. Fruit, meat, vegetables, flour for homemade bread. Well, shop bread is full of pollutants. Frozen food, even
110 your own, loses flavour. Martin often remarks on it. Condiments. Everyone loves mango chutney. But the expense!

London Airport to the left. Look, look, children! Concorde? No, idiot, of course it isn't Concorde.

Ah, to be all things to all people: children, husband, employer, friends!
115 It can be done: yes, it can: super woman.

Drink. Home-made wine. Why not? Elderberries, grown thick and rich in London: and at least you know what's in it. Store it in high cupboards: lots of room: up and down the step-ladder. Careful! Don't slip. Don't break anything.
120 No such thing as an accident. Accidents are Freudian slips: they are wilful, bad-tempered things.

Martin can't bear bad temper. Martin likes slim ladies. Diet. Martin rather likes his secretary. Diet. Martin admires slim legs and big bosoms. How to achieve them both? Impossible. But try, oh try, to be what you
125 ought to be, not what you are. Inside and out.

Martin brings back flowers and chocolates: whisks Martha off for holiday weekends. Wonderful! The best husband in the world: look into

87 drowse: be in a light sleep
88 tonsil: *Mandel*
89 molar: big tooth at the back of your mouth
89 confiscate sth.: take sth. away from sb. who is not allowed to have it
93 jolt sb. awake: tear sb. from sleep
101 seniority: higher rank
103 reward (n): sth. you receive as a compensation for sth. else
109 pollutant (fml): dangerous or poisonous substance
110 condiment: sth. (especially a sauce) added to your food to make it more tasty
111 expense: costs
120 Freudian slip: ['frɔɪdɪən] mistake that occurs because your subconscious interferes
121 wilful (fml): done deliberately
126 whisk sb. off: take sb. somewhere quickly

his crinkly, merry, gentle eyes; see it there. So the mouth slopes away into something of a pout. Never mind. Gaze into the eyes. Love. It must
130 be love. You married him. *You*. Surely *you* deserve true love?

Salisbury Plain. Stonehenge. Look, children, look! Mother, we've seen Stonehenge a hundred times. Go back to sleep.

Cook! Ah cook. People love to come to Martin and Martha's dinners. Work it out in your head in the lunch-hour. If you get in at six-twelve,
135 you can seal the meat while you beat the egg white while you feed the cat while you lay the table while you string the beans while you set out the cheese, goat's cheese, Martin loves goat's cheese, Martha tries to like goat's cheese – oh, bed, sleep, peace, quiet.

Sex! Ah sex. Orgasm, please. Martin requires it: Well, so do you. And
140 you don't want his secretary providing a passion you neglected to develop. Do you? Quick, quick, the cosmic bond. Love. Married love.

Secretary! Probably a vulgar suspicion: nothing more. Probably a fit of paranoics, à la mother, now dead and gone.

At peace. R.I.P.
145 Chilly, lonely mother, following her suspicions where they led.

Nearly there, children. Nearly in paradise, nearly at the cottage. Have another biscuit.

Real roses round the door.

Roses. Prune, weed, spray, feed, pick. Avoid thorns. One of
150 Martin's few harsh words.

'Martha, you can't not want roses! What kind of person am I married to? An anti-rose personality?'

Green grass. Oh, God, grass. Grass must be mowed. Restful lawns, daisies bobbing, buttercups glowing. Roses and grass
155 and books. Books.

'Please, Martin, do we have to have the two hundred books, mostly twenties' first editions, bought at Christie's book sale on one of your afternoons off? Books need dusting.

Roars of laughter from Martin, Jasper, Jenny and Jolyon. Mummy
160 says we shouldn't have the books: books need dusting!

Roses, green grass, books and peace.

Martha woke up with a start when they got to the cottage, and gave a little shriek which made them all laugh. Mummy's waking shriek, they called it.
165 Then there was the car to unpack and the beds to make up, and the electricity to connect, and the supper to make, and the cobwebs to remove, while Martin made the fire. Then supper – pork chops in sweet and sour sauce ('Pork is such a *dull* meat if you don't cook it properly': Martin), green salad from the garden, or such green salad as the rabbits
170 had left ('Martha, did you really net them properly? Be honest now!': Martin) and sauté potatoes. Mash is so stodgy and ordinary, and instant mash unthinkable. The children studied the night sky with the aid of their star map. Wonderful, rewarding children!

129 pout (n): facial expression in which you push your lips out in order to show displeasure
149 prune sth.: cut off parts of a plant so that it grows better and stronger
149 weed (v): remove wild plants from the ground to make room for garden plants
170 net sth.: cover sth. with a net
171 mash (n): boiled potatoes that have been mixed with butter and milk so as to create a soft mass
171 stodgy (BE, infml): making you feel full

Then clear up the supper: set the dough to prove for the bread: Martin
175 already in bed: exhausted by the drive and lighting the fire. ('Martha,
we really ought to get the logs stacked properly. Get the children to do
it, will you?': Martin) Sweep and tidy: get the TV aerial right. Turn up
Jasper's jeans where he has trodden the hem undone. ('He can't go
around like *that*, Martha. Not even Jasper': Martin)
180 Midnight. Good night. Weekend guests arriving in the morning.
Seven for lunch and dinner on Saturday. Seven for Sunday breakfast,
nine for Sunday lunch. ('Don't fuss, darling. You always make such a
fuss': Martin) Oh, God, forgotten the garlic squeezer. That means ten
minutes with the back of a spoon and salt. Well, who wants *lumps* of
185 garlic? No one. Not Martin's guests. Martin said so. Sleep.
Colin and Katie. Colin is Martin's oldest friend. Katie is his new young
wife. Janet, Colin's other, earlier wife, was Martha's friend.
Janet was rather like Martha, quieter and duller than her husband.
A nag and a drag, Martin rather thought, and said, and of course she'd
190 let herself go, everyone agreed. No one exactly excused Colin walking
out, but you could see the temptation.
Katie versus Janet.
Katie was languid, beautiful and elegant. She drawled when she
spoke. Her hands were expressive: her feet were little and female. She
195 had no children.
Janet plodded round on very flat, rather large feet. There was something wrong with them. They turned out slightly when she walked. She
had two children. She was, frankly, boring. But Martha liked her: when
Janet carne down to the cottage she would wash up. Not in the way
200 that most guests washed up – washing dutifully and setting everything
out on the draining board, but actually drying and putting away too.
And Janet would wash the bath and get the children all sat down, with
chairs for everyone, even the littlest, and keep them quiet and satisfied
so the grown-ups – well, the men – could get on with their conversation
205 and their jokes and their love of country weekends, while Janet stared
into space, as if grateful for the rest, quite happy.
Janet would garden, too. Weed the strawberries, while the men went
for their walk; her great feet standing firm and square and sometime
crushing a plant or so, but never mind, oh never mind. Lovely Janet;
210 who understood.
Now Janet was gone and here was Katie.
Katie talked with the men and went for walks with the men, and
moved her ashtray rather impatiently when Martha tried to clear the
drinks round it.
215 Dishes were boring, Katie implied by her manner, and domesticity
was boring, and anyone who bothered with that kind of thing was a
fool. Like Martha. Ash should be allowed to stay where it was, even if
it was in the butter, and conversations should never be interrupted.

174 prove: (of bread dough) grow in size and become fluffy before being baked
176 log: piece of wood
178 tread [tred] (trod – trodden): press sth. down with your feet
178 hem: *Saum*
178 undone: not fastened
188 dull: unexciting, not clever
189 nag (n): unpleasant person
189 drag (n, infml): boring person
193 languid: moving slowly in an attractive way
193 drawl (v): speak slowly, lengthening the vowels

Knock, knock. Katie and Colin arrived at one-fifteen on Saturday
220 morning, just after Martha had got to bed. 'You don't mind? It was the
moonlight. We couldn't resist it. You should have seen Stonehenge! We
didn't disturb you? Such early birds!'

Martha rustled up a quick meal of omelettes. Saturday night's eggs.
('Martha makes a lovely omelette': Martin) ('Honey, make one of your
225 mushroom omelettes: cook the mushrooms separately, remember, with
lemon. Otherwise the water from the mushrooms gets into the egg, and
spoils everything.') Sunday supper mushrooms. But ungracious to say
anything.

Martin had revived wonderfully at the sight of Colin and Katie. He
230 brought out the whisky bottle. Glasses. Ice. Jug for water. Wait. Wash
up another sinkful, when they're finished. 2 a.m.

'Don't do it tonight, darling.'

'It'll only take a sec.' Bright smile, not a hint of self-pity. Self-pity
can spoil everyone's weekend.

235 Martha knows that if breakfast for seven is to be manageable the
sink must be cleared of dishes. A tricky meal, breakfast. Especially if
bacon, eggs, and tomatoes must all be cooked in separate pans. ('Separate
pans mean separate flavours!': Martin)

She is running around in her nightie. Now if that had been Katie –
240 but there's something so *practical* about Martha. Reassuring, mind; but
the skimpy nightie and the broad rump and the thirty-eight years are
all rather embarrassing. Martha can see it in Colin and Katie's eyes.
Martin's too. Martha wishes she did not see so much in other people's
eyes. Her mother did, too. Dear, dead mother. Did I misjudge you?

245 This was the second weekend Katie had been down with Colin but
without Janet. Colin was a photographer: Katie had been his accessorizer. First Colin and Janet: then Colin, Janet and Katie: now Colin and
Katie!

Katie weeded with rubber gloves on and pulled out pansies in mistake
250 for weeds and laughed and laughed along with everyone when her
mistake was pointed out to her, but the pansies died. Well, Colin had
become with the years fairly rich and fairly famous, and what does a
fairly rich and famous man want with a wife like Janet when Katie is
at hand?

255 On the first of the Colin/Janet/Katie weekends Katie had appeared
out of the bathroom. 'I say,' said Katie, holding out a damp towel with
evident distaste, 'I can only find this. No hope of a dry one?' And Martha
had run to fetch a dry towel and amazingly found one, and handed it
to Katie who flashed her a brilliant smile and said, 'I can't bear damp
260 towels. Anything in the world but damp towels,' as if speaking to a
servant in a time of shortage of staff, and took all the water so there
was none left for Martha to wash up.

236 sink (n): basin in the kitchen in which you wash your dishes
241 skimpy: very small, leaving much of your body uncovered
241 rump: part of the body that you sit on
246 accessorizer: *Ausstatterin/Ausstatter*

51

The trouble, of course, was drying anything at all in the cottage. There were no facilities for doing so, and Martin had a horror of clothes
265 lines which might spoil the view. He toiled and moiled all week in the city simply to get a country view at the weekend. Ridiculous to spoil it by draping it with wet towels! But now Martha had bought more towels, so perhaps everyone could be satisfied. She would take nine damp towels back on Sunday evenings in a plastic bag and see to them in
270 London.

On this Saturday morning, straight after breakfast, Katie went out to the car – she and Colin had a new Lamborghini; hard to imagine Katie in anything duller – and came back waving a new Yves St Laurent towel. 'See! I brought my own, darlings.'
275 They'd brought nothing else. No fruit, no meat, no vegetables, not even bread, certainly not a box of chocolates. They'd gone off to bed with alacrity, the night before, and the spare room rocked and heaved: well, who'd want to do washing-up when you could do that, but what about the children? Would they get confused? First Colin and Janet,
280 now Colin and Katie?

Martha murmured something of her thoughts to Martin, who looked quite shocked. 'Colin's my best friend. I don't expect him to bring anything,' and Martha felt mean. 'And good heavens, you can't protect the kids from sex for ever: don't be so prudish,' so that Martha felt
285 stupid as well. Mean, complaining, and stupid.

Janet had rung Martha during the week. The house had been sold over her head, and she and the children had been moved into a small flat. Katie was trying to persuade Colin to cut down on her allowance, Janet said.
290 'It does one no good to be materialistic,' Katie confided. 'I have nothing. No home, no family, no ties, no possessions. Look at me! Only me and a suitcase of clothes.' But Katie seemed highly satisfied with the me, and the clothes were stupendous. Katie drank a great deal and became funny. Everyone laughed, including Martha. Katie had been
295 married twice. Martha marvelled at how someone could arrive in their midthirties with nothing at all to their name, neither husband, nor children, nor property and not mind.

Mind you, Martha could see the power of such helplessness. If Colin was all Katie had in the world, how could Colin abandon her? And to
300 what? Where would she go? How would she live? Oh, clever Katie.

'My teacup's dirty,' said Katie, and Martha ran to clean it, apologizing, and Martin raised his eyebrows, at Martha, not Katie.

'I wish *you'd* wear scent,' said Martin to Martha, reproachfully. Katie wore lots. Martha never seemed to have time to put any on, though.
305 Martin bought her bottle after bottle. Martha leapt out of bed each morning to meet some emergency – miaowing cat, coughing child,

265 toil, moil (v, fml): work very hard
272 Lamborghini: type of luxury car
273 Yves St Laurent: French luxury fashion company
277 alacrity: enthusiasm, cheerfulness
277 rock (v): (here) shake violently
277 heave (n): go up and down with strong movements
284 prudish: *prüde*
288 allowance: amount of money given to sb. on a regular basis
293 stupendous (infml): extremely impressive
303 scent: perfume
303 reproachful: expressing criticism or disapproval

faulty alarm dock, postman's knock – when was Martha to put on scent? It annoyed Martin all the same. She ought to do more to charm him.

Colin looked handsome and harrowed and younger than Martin,
310 though they were much the same age. 'Youth's catching,' said Martin in bed that night. 'It's since he found Katie.' Found, like some treasure. Discovered; something exciting and wonderful, in the dreary world of established spouses.

On Saturday morning Jasper trod on a piece of wood ('Martha, why
315 isn't he wearing shoes? It's too bad': Martin) and Martha took him into the hospital to have a nasty splinter removed. She left the cottage at ten and arrived back at one, and they were still sitting in the sun, drinking, empty bottles glinting in the long grass. The grass hadn't been cut. Don't forget the bottles. Broken glass means more mornings at the
320 hospital. Oh, don't fuss. Enjoy yourself. Like other people. Try.

But no potatoes peeled, no breakfast cleared, nothing. Cigarette ends still amongst old toast, bacon rind and marmalade. 'You could have done the potatoes,' Martha burst out. Oh, bad temper! Prime sin. They looked at her in amazement and dislike. Martin too.
325 'Goodness,' said Katie. 'Are we doing the whole Sunday lunch bit on Saturday? Potatoes? Ages since I've eaten potatoes. Wonderful!'

'The children expect it,' said Martha.

So they did. Saturday and Sunday lunch shone like reassuring beacons in their lives. Saturday lunch: family lunch: fish and chips. ('So
330 much better cooked at home than bought': Martin). Sunday. Usually roast beef, potatoes, peas, apple pie. Oh, of course. Yorkshire pudding. Always a problem with oven temperatures. When the beef's going slowly, the Yorkshire should be going fast. How to achieve that? Like big bosom and little hips.
335 'Just relax,' said Martin. 'I'll cook dinner, all in good time. Splinters always work their own way out: no need to have taken him to hospital. Let life drift over you, my love. Flow with the waves, that's the way.'

And Martin flashed Martha a distant, spiritual smile. His hand lay on Katie's slim brown arm, with its many gold bands.
340 'Anyway, you do too much for the children,' said Martin. 'It isn't good for them! Have a drink.'

So Martha perched uneasily on the step and had a glass of cider, and wondered how, if lunch was going to be late, she would get cleared up and the meat out of the marinade for the rather formal dinner that would
345 be expected that evening. The marinaded lamb ought to cook for at least four hours in a low oven; and the cottage oven was very small, and you couldn't use that and the grill at the same time and Martin liked his fish grilled, not fried. Less cholesterol.

She didn't say as much. Domestic details like this were very boring,
350 and any mild complaint was registered by Martin as a scene. And to make a scene was so ungrateful.

309 harrowed: tormented
313 spouse: wife or husband
316 splinter: small sharp piece of wood
337 drift (v): (here) pass smoothly and slowly

Roast beef with Yorkshire pudding

This was the life. Well, wasn't it? Smart friends in large cars and country living and drinks before lunch and roses and bird song 'Don't drink *too* much,' said Martin, and told them about Martha's suspended
355 driving licence.

The children were hungry so Martha opened them a can of beans and sausages and heated that up. ('Martha, do they have to eat that crap? Can't they wait?': Martin)

Katie was hungry: she said so, to keep the children in face. She was
360 lovely with children – most children. She did not particularly like Colin and Janet's children. She said so, and he accepted it. He only saw them once a month now, not once a week.

'Let me make lunch,' Katie said to Martha. 'You do so much, poor thing!'

365 And she pulled out of the fridge all the things Martha had put away for the next day's picnic lunch party – Camembert cheese and salad and salami and made a wonderful tomato salad in two minutes and opened the white wine – 'not very cold, darling. Shouldn't it be chilling?' and had it all on the table in five amazing competent minutes. 'That's all we
370 need, darling,' said Martin. 'You are funny with your fish-and-chip Saturdays! What could be nicer than this? Or simpler?'

Nothing, except there was Sunday's buffet lunch for nine gone, in place of Saturday's fish for six, and would the fish stretch? No. Katie had had quite a lot to drink. She pecked Martha on the forehead. 'Funny
375 little Martha,' she said. 'She reminds me of Janet. I really do like Janet.' Colin did not want to be reminded of Janet, and said so. 'Darling, Janet's a fact of life,' said Katie. 'If you'd only think about her more, you might manage to pay her less.' And she yawned and stretched her lean, child-less body and smiled at Colin with her inviting, naughty little girl eyes,
380 and Martin watched her in admiration.

Martha got up and left them and took a paint pot and put a coat of white gloss on the bathroom wall. The white surface pleased her. She was good at painting. She produced a smooth, even surface. Her legs throbbed. She feared she might be getting varicose veins.

385 Outside in the garden the children played badminton. They were bad-tempered, but relieved to be able to look up and see their mother working, as usual: making their lives for ever better and nicer; organizing, planning, thinking ahead, side-stepping disaster, making preparations, like a mother hen, fussing and irritating: part of the natural
390 boring scenery of the world.

On Saturday night Katie went to bed early: she rose from her chair and stretched and yawned and poked her head into the kitchen where Martha was washing saucepans. Colin had cleared the table and Katie had folded the napkins into pretty creases, while Martin blew at the
395 fire, to make it bright. 'Good night,' said Katie.

384 varicose vein: swollen and painful blood vessel, especially in your leg
389 fuss (v): complain, worry about things that aren't really important
389 irritate sb.: annoy sb.

Katie appeared three minutes later, reproachfully holding out her Yves St Laurent towel, sopping wet. 'Oh dear,' cried Martha. 'Jenny must have washed her hair!' And Martha was obliged to rout Jenny out of bed to rebuke her, publicly, if only to demonstrate that she knew
400 what was right and proper. That meant Jenny would sulk all weekend, and that meant a treat or an outing mid-week, or else by the following week she'd be having an asthma attack. 'You fuss the children too much,' said Martin. 'That's why Jenny has asthma.' Jenny was pleasant enough to look at, but not stunning. Perhaps she was a disappointment to her
405 father? Martin would never say so, but Martha feared he thought so.

An egg and an orange each child, each day. Then nothing too bad would go wrong. And it hadn't. The asthma was very mild. A calm, tranquil environment, the doctor said. Ah, smile, Martha smile. Domestic happiness depends on you. 21 x 52 oranges a year. Each one to be
410 purchased, carried, peeled and washed up after. And what about potatoes. 12 x 52 pounds a year? Martin liked his potatoes carefully peeled. He couldn't bear to find little cores of black in the mouthful. ('Well, it isn't very nice, is it?': Martin).

Martha dreamt she was eating coal, by handfuls, and liking it.

415 Saturday night. Martin made love to Martha three times. Three times? How virile he was, and clearly turned on by the sounds from the spare room. Martin said he loved her. Martin always did. He was a courteous lover; he knew the importance of foreplay. So did Martha. Three times.

420 Ah, sleep. Jolyon had a nightmare. Jenny was woken by a moth. Martin slept through everything. Martha pottered about the house in the night. There was a moon. She sat at the window and stared out into the summer night for five minutes, and was at peace, and then went back to bed because she ought to be fresh for the morning.

425 But she wasn't. She slept late. The others went out for a walk. They'd left a note, a considerate note: 'Didn't wake you. You looked tired. Had a cold breakfast so as not to make too much mess. Leave everything 'til we get back.' But it was ten o'clock, and guests were coming at noon, so she cleared away the bread, the butter, the crumbs, the smears, the
430 jam, the spoons, the spilt sugar, the cereal, the milk (sour now) and the dirty plates, and swept the floors, and tidied up quickly, and grabbed a cup of coffee, and prepared to make a rice and fish dish, and a chocolate mousse and sat down in the middle to eat a lot of bread and jam herself. Broad hips. She remembered the office work in her file and knew she
435 wouldn't be able to do it. Martin anyway thought it was ridiculous for her to bring work back at the weekends. 'It's your holiday,' he'd say. 'Why should they impose?' Martha loved her work. She didn't have to smile at it. She just did it.

Katie came back upset and crying. She sat in the kitchen while
440 Martha worked and drank glass after glass of gin and bitter lemon. Katie

404 stunning (infml): extremely attractive
437 impose: expect sb. to do sth., especially sth. inconvenient

liked ice and lemon in gin. Martha paid for all the drink out of her wages. It was part of the deal between her and Martin – the contract by which she went out to work. All things to cheer the spirit, otherwise depressed by a working wife and mother, were to be paid for by Martha. Drink,
445 holidays, petrol, outings, puddings, electricity, heating: it was quite a joke between them. It didn't really make any difference: it was their joint money, after all. Amazing how Martha's wages were creeping up almost to the level of Martin's. One day they would overtake. Then what?

450 Work, honestly, was a piece of cake.

Anyway, poor Katie was crying: Colin, she'd discovered, kept a photograph of Janet and the children in his wallet. 'He's not free of her. He pretends he is, but he isn't. She has him by a stranglehold. It's the kids. His bloody kids. Moaning Mary and that little creep Joanna. It's all he
455 thinks about. I'm nobody.'

But Katie didn't believe it. She knew she was somebody all right. Colin came in, in a fury. He took out the photograph and set fire to it, bitterly, with a match. Up in smoke they went. Mary and Joanna and Janet. The ashes fell on the floor. (Martha swept them up when Colin
460 and Katie had gone. It hardly seemed polite to do so when they were still there.) 'Go back to her,' Katie said. 'Go back to her. I don't care. Honestly, I'd rather be on my own. You're a nice old fashioned thing. Run along then. Do your thing, I'll do mine. Who cares?'

'Christ, Katie, the fuss! She only just happens to be in the photograph.
465 She's not there on purpose to annoy. And I do feel bad about her. She's been having a hard time.'

'And haven't you, Colin? She twists a pretty knife, I can tell you. Don't you have rights too? Not to mention me. Is a little loyalty too much to expect?'

470 They were reconciled before lunch, up in the spare room. Harry and Beryl Elder arrived at twelve-thirty. Harry didn't like to hurry on Sundays; Beryl was flustered with apologies for their lateness. They'd brought artichokes from their garden. 'Wonderful,' cried Martin. 'Fruits of the earth? Let's have a wonderful soup! Don't fret, Martha. I'll do it.'
475 'Don't fret.' Martha clearly hadn't been smiling enough. She was in danger, Martin implied, of ruining everyone's weekend. There was an emergency in the garden very shortly – an elm tree which had probably got Dutch elm disease – and Martha finished the artichokes. The lid flew off the blender and there was artichoke purée everywhere. 'Let's have
480 lunch outside,' said Colin. 'Less work for Martha.'

Martin frowned at Martha: he thought the appearance of martyrdom in the face of guests to be an unforgivable offence.

Everyone happily joined in taking the furniture out, but it was Martha's experience that nobody ever helped to bring it in again.

---

453 have sb. by a stranglehold: have complete control over sb.
454 moan (infml): complain about sth. in an annoying way
454 creep (n): highly unpleasant person
472 fluster sb.: make sb. nervous or confused
482 offence: highly inappropriate behaviour

485   Jolyon was stung by a wasp. Jasper sneezed and sneezed from hay fever and couldn't find the tissues and he wouldn't use loo paper. ('Surely you remembered the tissues, darling?': Martin)

    Beryl Elder was nice. 'Wonderful to eat out,' she said, fetching the cream for her pudding, while Martha fished a fly from the liquefying

490 Brie ('You shouldn't have bought it so ripe, Martha': Martin) – 'except it's just some other woman has to do it. But at least it isn't *me*.' Beryl worked too, as a secretary, to send the boys to boarding school, where she'd rather they weren't. But her husband was from a rather grand family, and she'd been only a typist when he married her, so her life

495 was a mass of amends, one way or another. Harry had lately opted out of the stockbroking rat race and become an artist, choosing integrity rather than money, but that choice was his alone and couldn't of course be inflicted on the boys.

    Katie found the fish and rice dish rather strange, toyed at it with her

500 fork, and talked about Italian restaurants she knew. Martin lay back soaking in the sun: crying, 'Oh, this is the life.' He made coffee, nobly, and the lid flew off the grinder and there were coffee beans all over the kitchen especially in amongst the row of cookery books which Martin gave Martha Christmas by Christmas. At least they didn't have to be

505 brought back every weekend. ('The burglars won't have the sense to steal those': Martin)

    Beryl fell asleep and Katie watched her, quizzically. Beryl's mouth was open and she had a lot of fillings, and her ankles were thick and her waist was going, and she didn't look after herself. 'I love women,' sighed Katie.

510 'They look so wonderful asleep. I wish I could be an earth mother.'

    Beryl woke with a start and nagged her husband into going home, which he clearly didn't want to do, so didn't. Beryl thought she had to get back because his mother was coming round later. Nonsense! Then Beryl tried to stop Harry drinking more home-made wine and was

515 laughed at by everyone. He was driving, Beryl couldn't, and he did have a nasty scar on his temple from a previous road accident. Never mind.

    'She does come on strong, poor soul,' laughed Katie when they'd finally gone. 'I'm never going to get married,' – and Colin looked at her yearningly because he wanted to marry her more than anything in the

520 world, and Martha cleared the coffee cups.

    'Oh don't *do* that,' said Katie, 'do just sit *down*, Martha, you make us all feel bad,' and Martin glared at Martha who sat down and Jenny called out for her and Martha went upstairs and Jenny had started her first period and Martha cried and cried and knew she must stop because

525 this must be a joyous occasion for Jenny or her whole future would be blighted, but for once, Martha couldn't.

    Her daughter Jenny: wife, mother, friend.

From: Susan Hill, ed., The Penguin Book of Modern Women's Short Stories, *1990; first published in 1978*

---

489 liquefy ['lɪkwɪfaɪ]: become liquid
495 amends (pl): effort to make up for sth.
495 opt out of sth.: choose to leave sth.
496 stockbroking: business of buying and selling shares of companies
496 rat race: highly competitive way of life of people living in the city and competing in an aggressive way for wealth and influence
498 inflict sth. on sb.: make sb. suffer something unpleasant
511 nag sb. into doing sth.: keep asking sb. to do sth.

Info Fay Weldon

Fay Weldon, born as Franklin Birkinshaw in Birmingham, England, in 1931, grew up in Christchurch, New Zealand. Returning to England with her mother and sister in 1946 after her parents' divorce, she attended a girls' school before studying Economics and Psychology at the University of St Andrews, Scotland. After her M.A. degree she moved to London and took up a position at the Foreign Office writing pamphlets as part of the Cold War effort. When she became pregnant she had to leave this job and worked in advertising to support herself and her son as a single mother. She started writing for radio and television and her first novel, *The Fat Woman's Joke*, was published in 1967. Over the course of her career Weldon wrote 31 novels, numerous short stories, plays, essays, radio and television scripts and became well-known as an outspoken, often controversial public figure.

Weldon started out with a focus on the problems women face. Her aim was to make their voices heard and to question gender roles and power relations between the sexes. Later, she also addressed a wide range of other issues in her writing (among them Islam, rape, therapy, the role of the author). Although she saw herself as a feminist writer trying to promote social change, she was not afraid to criticize aspects of feminism that she disagreed with, always encouraging women to take responsibility for their own lives. She died in January 2023.

Comprehension

1 Tick the correct answer and find a suitable quote from the text.

a The car has been packed for the weekend by …
    A Martin.
    B Martha.
    C the three children.
    D Martin and Martha.

line: _____
quote: _____

b In Martin's view Martha should …
    A run the house herself.
    B allow him to pay for the cleaning.
    C pay for the cleaning lady.
    D ask the children to do more housework.

line: _____
quote: _____

c Martha lost her driving license because she …
    A was caught speeding.
    B hit another car.
    C fell asleep at the wheel.
    D was drunk.

line: _____
quote: _____

d Martin dislikes Martha's car and complains
because it is …
   A small.
   B full of stuff.
   C not his.

line: _____

quote: _____

e When Martha says she does not like the way
he speaks about the car, Martin …
   A gets angry.
   B does not take her seriously.
   C denies it.
   D ignores her.

line: _____

quote: _____

f Returning to work after having had children
Martha gets …
   A a new job at a different agency.
   B her old job back.
   C a better job at her old agency.
   D a less well-paid job at her old agency.

line: _____

quote: _____

g Martin prefers women to be …
   A curvy with thin legs.
   B tall with dark hair.
   C skinny with long legs.
   D boyish with round lips.

line: _____

quote: _____

h When having sex with Martin, Martha …
   A is passionate.
   B rather enjoys it.
   C feels under pressure.
   D is indifferent.

line: _____

quote: _____

i Martin …
   A understands why Colin left Janet.
   B cannot understand why Colin left Janet.
   C criticizes Colin for leaving Janet.
   D feels tempted by Colin's new wife.

line: _____

quote: _____

j Katie and Colin spontaneously arrive …
   A after breakfast.
   B late on Saturday morning.
   C in the middle of the night.
   D just before breakfast.

line: _____

quote: _____

k Running around in her nightdress Martha
feels …

  A reassured.

  B sexy.

  C carefree.

  D self-conscious.

line: _____

quote: _____

l When Colin and Katie have noisy sex,
Martha is bothered because she …

  A envies them.

  B doesn't want to talk about it with Martin.

  C feels prudish.

  D doesn't want the children to hear them.

line: _____

quote: _____

m When Martin asks Martha to wear more
scent she …

  A does it to please him.

  B thinks she does not have the time.

  C says she does not like it.

  D uses some of Katie's.

line: _____

quote: _____

n Because of Katie, Colin …

  A moves to a small flat.

  B pays his wife less allowance.

  C visits Martin only rarely.

  D sees his children more seldom than before.

line: _____

quote: _____

o Martha's fusses a lot about her children.
The children …

  A take this for granted.

  B are happy about this.

  C are thankful for this.

  D resent this.

line: _____

quote: _____

p When the others go for a walk on Sunday
morning, they …

  A leave a cold breakfast for Martha.

  B leave Martha with all the clearing up to do.

  C expect Martha to follow them.

  D promise to be back by ten.

line: _____

quote: _____

2 Create three more multiple choice questions for the final part of the
story (l. 438 ff.) and test your classmate's understanding of the story.

Analysis

3 a Work in three groups and re-read different passages from the text:
Group 1: l. 1 – l. 160
Group 2: l. 161 – l. 312
Group 3: l. 313 – l. 526.
List and compare the things Martin and Martha do for the family
and their friends.

Martin	Martha

b State what this tells you about their relationship.

4 Martha often worries about things Martin says because she suspects
an implied message.

a Look at the examples below and write down what Martin might
actually mean.

What Martin says ...	What Martin might mean ...
'... you ought to get Mrs Hodder to do more. She takes advantage of you.' (l. 28)	– *The house is not clean enough.* – *Martha is not coping with all the housework.* – *Martha is not handling the staff well.*
A 'Pork is such a dull meat if you don't cook it properly.' (l. 167)	
B '... did you net them properly? Be honest now.' (l. 169)	
C '... we really ought to get the logs stacked properly. Get the children to do it, will you?' (l. 175)	

What Martin says ...	What Martin might mean ...
D 'He can't go around like that, Martha. Not even Jasper.' (l. 177)	
E 'Don't fuss, darling. You always make such a fuss.' (l. 181)	
F 'Martha makes a lovely omelette' (l. 223)	
G 'Don't do it tonight, darling.' (l. 231)	
H 'Colin's my best friend. I don't expect him to bring anything[.]' (l. 281)	
I 'Youth's catching ... It's since he found Katie.' (l. 311)	
J '... why isn't he wearing shoes?' (l. 313)	
K 'Don't drink too much[.]' (l. 352)	
L 'Martha, do they have to eat that crap?' (l. 356)	

  b Analyse the way Martin communicates to get his intentions across.

5 Examine Martha's attitude to her family and friends, to herself and her life in general.

6 Contrast the couple's two cars. State what they tell us about their drivers.

7 **a** Compare the female characters in the story.
   b State which of the women comes closest to Martin's idea of femininity and why.

8 Explain the last sentence of the story.

9 Examine the author's use of narrative perspective ($\rightarrow$ Info box, p. 63).

> **Info Narrative perspective**
> The narrator of a story can be a character of the story, or a nameless voice that tells the story without taking part in it. A **first-person narrator** refers to him- or herself as 'I' and tells the story from their own point of view. First-person narration is always connected with a limited point of view. Alternatively, a story can be told in the **third person**. In this case, the narrator is a nameless voice that doesn't belong to the plot. The narrator may, however, have a **limited point of view**, i. e. the narrator only knows and sees what one particular character knows and sees (single-character point of view). In a longer text, the narrative perspective may jump from one character to another (**multiple-character point of view**). In traditional novels, the narrator is often an independent voice that stands above the action and thus has an **unlimited point of view**.

Beyond the text

10 `Speaking` On the following day, Martha and her daughter talk. Act out their dialogue.

11 `Writing` Re-write a part of the story from another character's perspective (e.g. one of the children, one of the guests, Martin). Present your stories in class and discuss in what way this changes the story.

12 `Writing` What might happen if the story took place today and Martha was the breadwinner of the family and Martin took care of the household? Re-write (a part of) the story, then present your texts to class and compare them.

13 `Speaking` At some stage, Martha has had enough and considers a divorce. She talks to a family lawyer. Act out their dialogue.

14 a Discuss what might happen if …
  – Martha quit her job?
  – Martin lost his job?
  – Martha met someone else?

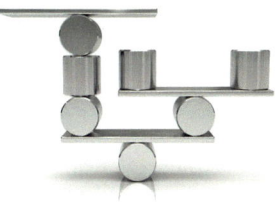

b Imagine other scenarios in which the power balance between Martha and Martin might shift. Describe what might happen.

15 If a good fairy came in the night to take away all Martha's problems, what would change? How would Martha behave? What would she notice? How would the people around her react? Make a list and explain your ideas.

16 Find an image to illustrate the story. Justify your choice in a short text.

17 Women are complicit in a system in which men have power over women. Discuss.

18 Martha has both, a family and a career. Would you consider her a modern, emancipated woman? Give reasons.

19 Authors have the opportunity and a responsibility to instigate change. Discuss.

Part C
Post-reading activities

C1 'We Should All Be Feminists'

Chimamanda Ngozi Adichie

1 **a** What might people aspire to in their lives? Collect ideas.
   b Which of these aspirations would traditionally be associated with women, which of them with men? Discuss.
2 What makes a person a feminist? Discuss your ideas with a partner.

Info Chimamanda Ngozi Adichie

Chimamanda Ngozi Adichie (born 1977) is a Nigerian writer whose first book, *Purple Hibiscus* (2003) became a worldwide success. She grew up in the city of Nsukka and first started studying medicine and pharmacy at the University of Nigeria, where she also edited a student magazine. When she was 19 years old, she moved to the USA to study communications and political science. In 2003 she completed a master's degree in creative writing at Johns Hopkins University. From 2005–2006, she was a Hodder fellow at Princeton University. Adichie then went on to complete a second master's degree in African Studies at Yale University. Known for her feminist views, Adichie has written many other successful works, such as the novels *Half of a Yellow Sun* (2006) and *Americanah* (2013), the short story collection *The Thing Around Your Neck* (2009) and the essay 'We should all be feminists' (2014). She holds sixteen honorary doctorate degrees from some of the world's best universities. She divides her time between the USA and Nigeria, where she teaches writing workshops.

Comprehension

3 Listen to a part of Chimamanda Ngozie Adichie's 2012 TED talk 'We should all be feminists'.

   Listening Complete the table below using information from the talk.

cornelsen.de
Code: bexupi

   A Why Adichie is angry

   B Why Adichie is also hopeful

   C Why she concentrates on Africa

D What the starting point for change might be

E What boys are taught today (2 aspects)

F What happens if a girl and a boy go out

G The worst effect of 'hard men' on boys

H The worst effects of 'hard men' on girls (2 aspects)

I Why Adichie is not worried about intimidating men

J What Adichie considers an advantage of marriage (2 aspects)

K What society thinks of an unmarried woman

L What society thinks of an unmarried man

M What 'for peace in my marriage' means for men

N What 'for peace in my marriage' means for women

O What society thinks of women

P What society thinks of men

Q How girls are taught to be as women

R The problem with gender

S What has changed since the times of
her grandmother (2 aspects)

Analysis
4 Examine how Adichie makes her talk interesting.
5 Come back to your ideas about feminists from **C1**, task **2** and
compare them to what you have seen of the talk.

Beyond the text
6 Comment on Adichie's idea that aspiring to marriage is expected of
women and that it changes their behaviour. Support your view with
examples (from films, books or real life).
7 The full TED talk is about 30 minutes long. Discuss if you'd like to
watch the complete version after seeing this extract.
8 **Writing** The book version of Adichie's talk was given to all
16-year-olds in Sweden in December 2015 to start a discussion
about gender equality. Write a comment on this approach.
9 **Speaking** Prepare your own 5-min TED talk about gender, equality
and/or feminism.
10 Imagine Martha or another character from the short story watching
the TED Talk. Work on either **a** or **b**.
  a **Speaking** Choose one character, then write their interior
  monologue.
  b **Writing** With a partner, act out their dialogue.

C2 Wrapping up: short stories

1 a In the table below, features found in most short stories are listed. Of the short stories you read, choose two and analyse which of the features apply to them. Make notes in the table. If the story you read does not include a specific feature, leave the space in the table blank.

Features	Title: _____	Title: _____
length (can be read in one sitting)		
direct start		
limited number of characters		
focus on one character/situation/dilemma/problem		
focus on one single aspect which undergoes a change during the story		

b Based on your results in **a**, state whether you'd classify the two stories as typical short stories.

2 Consider the women in the short stories from this collection that you've dealt with. Where would you place them on the following scale indicating their adjustment to the society that surrounds them? Give reasons.

<-- conformity   individualism -->

3 a Explain how the concepts on the right are dealt with in the short stories you've read.

b Speaking In pairs or groups, find three aspects or perspectives you would want to add. Collect materials that might be suitable to close the gap (songs, poems, short stories, film clips, cartoons, photos, …). Present your ideas to the class and justify your choices.

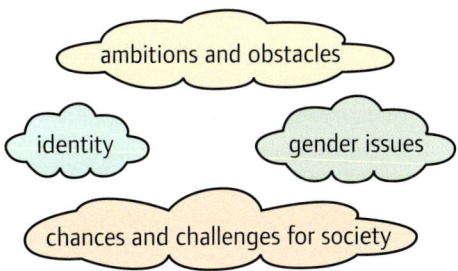

ambitions and obstacles

identity

gender issues

chances and challenges for society

A Midsummer Night's Dream

Part A
Pre-reading activities

A1 The Bard of Avon

Info William Shakespeare

William Shakespeare (1564–1616) is widely regarded as the greatest writer in the English language. He was born and brought up in Stratford-upon-Avon, England, where he married and had three children. He then moved to London, where, by 1592, he had
5   become known as a playwright and was beginning his acting career in the city's theatres. In 1594 he formed the Lord Chamberlain's Men with a group of actors, which soon became the leading theatre company in London. In 1599 they built their own theatre, the Globe, on the south bank of the River Thames. After the death of Queen Elizabeth I in 1603,
10   the company was awarded a royal patent by King James I and changed its name to the King's Men.

The famous Chandos portrait of William Shakespeare, named after the Dukes of Chandos, who owned the painting

Shakespeare produced most of his known works between 1589 and 1613. His early plays were mainly comedies and histories. Until about 1608 he wrote primarily tragedies, which were then followed by romances. *A Midsummer Night's Dream* was written in 1595 or 1596

15 and is considered one of his most original and beloved comedies. In 1623 two of his former colleagues published the *First Folio*, a collection of his dramatic works that included all but two of his plays. His sonnets were published in 1609.

Shakespeare appears to have retired to Stratford around 1613 at age 49. He died three years later. Few records of his private life survive, and there has been much speculation about his

20 physical appearance, sexuality, religious beliefs, and whether the works attributed to him were written by others. His surviving works consist of about 38 plays, 154 sonnets and several other poems. His plays are performed worldwide more often than those of any other playwright.

1 a Research the following topics:

> Elizabeth I and her time

> the original Globe Theatre

> Shakespeare's theatre troupes

> Shakespeare's family and education

> Shakespeare's comedies

> Shakespeare's Stratford

> Shakepeare's other plays

> Elizabethan theatre

> Renaissance London

b `Speaking` Present your findings to the class.

2 a Go online and research the Elizabethan Midsummer Night celebrations.

b Your school's project week this year is about classical literature and the Elizabethan era. Using your research from **a**, create a podcast or short video in which you explain the Midsummer Night celebrations.

A2 Lord, what fools these mortals be!

1 a `Viewing` Using the webcode on the right, go online and watch the TED-Ed video 'Why should you read *A Midsummer Night's Dream?'*. Outline the most important themes of the comedy put forward in this interpretation.

www.cornelsen.de
code: naqici

b With a partner, discuss whether the short film from **a** inspires you to read the play.

A3 Love and marriage

1 a Research the circumstances of Shakespeare's own marriage online and state which category of marriage (→ Info box) suits his situation.

b In four groups, discuss the advantages and downsides the concepts of love marriages and arranged marriages have for a couple, a family and society. Present your arguments to the class.

c Today, matchmaking apps or websites are hugely popular. Explain why people choose to find a partner online and discuss whether you think it's a good idea.

> **Info Arranged marriages**
> Marrying for love is a relatively new concept. For many centuries, matchmaking and arranging marriages for their children was the parents' privilege. In many societies worldwide, arranged marriages are still common. There are different types of arranged marriages: **forced marriages**, where bride and groom have no say in the matter due to social conventions; **child marriages** (also called early marriages), where at least one of the two people is not of adult age; and **pragmatic marriages**, where the partners have agreed to the pairing a matchmaker or parent has chosen.

A4 Away with the fairies

Reading Read the info box on the Elizabethans' beliefs about fairies and complete task 1 on p. 71.

> **Info Elizabethans' beliefs about fairies**
> In Shakespeare's time, people were very superstitious about nature and believed that ghosts and witches existed. They also thought that the world was full of good and bad spirits. Midsummer Night (June 20th or 21st) was seen as a potentially dangerous date because a portal between the real world and the fairy world would open up.
> 5 One fairy or goblin, Robin Goodfellow or Puck, was especially feared, as he loved to play practical, sometimes cruel jokes on humans. Some of the common beliefs were that fairies:
> • were active from midnight to dawn,
> • were invisible to humans and tiny (could hide in an acorn cup),
> • lived in a kingdom of their own,
> 10 • could take on a human form and make humans fall in love with them,
> • stole children and put fairy children in their places,
> • could lead people astray in the woods or cause minor accidents at home,
> • could change the weather and let fruit and vegetables rot,
> • could cause mischief in households by upsetting objects and interfering with cooking
> 15 and/or food preservation.
> People believed they could prevent such fairy pranks by carrying a lucky charm, keeping the house clean and leaving food and drinks for the spirits.

R O B I N
GOOD-FELLOW,
HIS MAD PRANKES AND
MERRY IESTS.

Full of honeſt Mirth, and is a fit Medicine
for Melancholy.

Printed at *London* by *Thomas Cotes*, and are to be fold by
Francis Groue, at his fhop on Snow-hil…..eere the

*Title Page of Robin Goodfellow
1639 edition*

1 **a** Study the woodcutting on the right that shows Puck on the title page of *Robin Goodfellow: His Mad Prankes and Merry Jests* (1639). Describe how he is depicted.

b The 2022 Oxford Dictionaries Word of the Year is 'goblin mode'. Look up its definition and discuss in which way modern people also behave 'puckishly'.

c Think of representations of fairies and elves in modern literature and in films, and compare them to Puck's illustration on the right.

2 Explain why many people might even believe in the supernatural today.

A5 Speak the speech, I pray you

1 Shakespeare wrote his plays mostly in blank verse, i.e. verses with a regular rhythm of ten beats, sometimes eleven, and no rhyme.

a Viewing Using the webcode on the right, go online and watch the TED-Ed video 'Why Shakespeare Loved Iambic Pentameter'.

b Speaking Work in teams. Applying what you learned in the video from **a**, take turns reading the following lines from *A Midsummer Night's Dream* out loud. Correct each other if needed.

 www.cornelsen.de
code: xusoga

'Full of vexation come I, with complaint
against my child, my daughter Hermia.' (Act I, Scene 1, ll. 22–23)

'O, teach me how you look, and with what art
you sway the motion of Demetrius' heart.' (Act I, Scene 1, ll. 192–193)

'The King doth keep his revels here tonight.
Take heed the Queen come not within his sight.' (Act II, Scene 1, ll. 18–19)

'What hast thou done? Thou hast mistaken quite
and laid the love juice on some true love's sight.' (Act III, Scene 2, ll. 88–89)

'What? Can you do me greater harm than hate?
Hate me? Wherefore? O me, what news, my love?' (Act III, Scene 2, ll. 271–272)

'Thou runaway, thou coward, art thou fled?
Speak! In some bush? Where dost thou hide thy head?' (Act III, Scene 2, ll. 405–406)

'The iron tongue of midnight hath told twelve.
Lovers, to bed; 'tis almost fairy time.' (Act V, Scene 1, ll. 345–346)

Part B
While-reading activities

B1 An unruly daughter (Act I, Scene 1)

Theseus, Duke of Athens, and his bride Hippolyta, Queen of the Amazons, are talking about the remaining four days before their upcoming wedding, for which the duke wants entertainment to be prepared. They are interrupted by Egeus, a prominent citizen, who asks for Theseus' judgment on an important matter.

Comprehension

1 Read ll. 20–127 and complete the sentences below.

A Egeus accuses Lysander of _____ .

B Egeus asks Theseus to _____ .

C Hermia argues that _____ .

D Theseus tells Hermia that _____

_____

E Hermia says she would rather _____ than _____ .

F Lysander accuses Demetrius of _____ .

2 Using the box on the right, draw arrows to show who loved whom before the play begins.

3 Identify the lines in the text in which …

A Hermia wants to know what happens if she disobeys her father.

B Theseus gives Hermia a deadline for her decision about her future.

C Lysander says he is in every way as suitable to be Hermia's future husband as Demetrius.

4 Read the rest of the scene and complete the sentences below. Don't forget the sentences on the next page.

A Hermia and Lysander list troubles that _____ .

B Their secret plan is to _____ .

Who loves whom?	
Before the play	
Hermia	Helena
Lysander	Demetrius

C Helena complains that Demetrius _____.

D Hermia assures Helena that _____.

E To make Helena feel better, Lysander and Hermia _____.

F When Helena is alone, she decides _____.

_____

Analysis

5 With a partner, take turns reading Hermia and Helena's dialogue in ll. 194–201. Examine the stylistic devices used and point out their intended effect on the reader.

6 Analyse the means Shakespeare uses to characterise the protagonists of this scene.

Beyond the text

7 Theseus and Hippolyta are figures from classical mythology, but in this excerpt they are presented as living characters. Comment on the dramatic reasons why Shakespeare might have made this decision.

8 **a** Hippolyta says very little during this emotional controversy about a girl's unhappy future. In a short monologue, imagine what she might say to Theseus about the situation and his judgment.

  b Speaking Present your speech to the class.

9 **a** With a partner, think about Hermia's, Lysander's and Helena's decisions and imagine possible outcomes for their intended actions. Discuss which arguments could convince them to find other solutions for their problems.

  b Share your findings from **a** with the class.

10 Discuss reasons why Demetrius might want to steal Lysander's girlfriend other than being in love with Hermia.

11 **a** Writing Write the diary entry Hermia might write on the day before she leaves her home. Take into account what happened while she was in the palace.

  b Writing Write the interior monologue Helena might go into when she debates with herself whether it is right or wrong to betray her best friend. State why she finally opts for telling Demetrius about Hermia's flight.

B2 Stagestruck (Act I, Scene 2)

Reading Read Scene 2 and complete tasks 1–8.

Comprehension

1 Imagine Tom Snout's wife asks him about the meeting of the amateur actors. From Snout's perspective, sum up what happened for her.

Analysis

2 Analyse the means Shakespeare uses to characterise the workmen, or 'Mechanicals'. Illustrate your findings by giving examples of their vocabulary and manner of speaking.

3 Explain whether you think Quince or Bottom has the higher status in this scene. Give evidence from the text.

> **Language help**
> diplomatic · self-confident · clever · ignorant · warm-hearted · easily led · boastful · enthusiastic · blundering [ˈblʌndə(r) ɪŋ] · subtle [ˈsʌtl] · conceited · firm · self-willed · resentful · modest · reluctant · energetic · sulky [ˈsʌlki] · overbearing · indifferent · uneducated · resourceful · determined · timid · incorrect · practical · vain · egoistic

4 Contrast Scenes 1 and 2 of Act I.

Beyond the text

5 Based on what you found in **4**, comment on the dramatic effect both scenes have on the audience.

6 Outline the plot you would suggest for the following scene if you could choose how the play continues.

7 a Viewing Watch the segment of the film *A Midsummer Night's Dream* (1999) from 00:14:36–00:22:35. Describe the choices Michael Hoffman made to represent Bottom.

b Evaluate the effect that is achieved.

c Comment on whether you find the interpretation of this segment convincing.

d Find pictures online of other actors playing Nick Bottom, e.g. Matt Lucas, Malcolm Storry, Marc Wootton or Hammed Animashaun. Compare their casting to Kevin Kline's. Suggest other actors for the role and justify your choices.

Actor Kevin Kline at a 2004 film screening in Beverly Hills, USA

8 a Writing Write the 'bill of properties' (l. 84–85) Peter Quince needs to prepare for the next rehearsal. Imagine the objects and costumes the play might need and list them individually for each actor.

b Speaking Imagine the slogans Nick Bottom would want to have printed on the front and back of his new T-shirt to advertise himself and the show, and what he would tell the printer about his new role. Write the speech using Bottom's way of speaking and present it to the class.

B3 Looking back on Act I

1 Examine the state of conflict shown in each relationship in the first scene of this act.
2 Discuss what you think about Theseus' ruling and find positive and negative aspects in his behaviour and decisions.
3 a **Think:** Note down what makes a good relationship between parent and child.
  b **Pair:** `Speaking` In small groups, put together a list of dos and don'ts you think are important.
  c **Share:** `Speaking` Share your findings in class and add new dos and don'ts you hear to your list from **b**.

B4 Overview (Act II, Scene 1, ll. 1–59)

Act II, Scene 1, ll. 1–59

In the forest around the Athenian palace, fairies appear at night and discuss a severe conflict in Fairyland. Puck, a goblin, tells a fairy that his master Oberon, King of the Fairies, is angry at his wife, Titania, because she refuses to give him a changeling child as a servant. The Queen of the Fairies wants to raise the boy herself. The fairy recognizes Puck as a mischievous goblin who likes to play pranks on mortals, which he enjoys telling her about. Both are displeased that the fairy royals will soon meet there by accident.

B5 Trouble in Fairyland (Act II, Scene 1, ll. 60–176)

Comprehension

1 Read ll. 60–80 of Act II, Scene 1. Tick the correct answer. Support your answer with lines from the text.

a During the fairy couple's conversation Titania …	Line(s):
A accuses Oberon of being unfaithful.	
B asks the fairies to stay and protect her.	_____
C criticizes Oberon for wanting to steal the changeling boy.	
b Oberon says that …	Line(s):
A he wants Titania to leave immediately.	
B Titania herself had an affair with another man.	_____
C he no longer considers himself Titania's husband.	

2 Now read ll. 81–117 of the scene. In her speech, Titania lists changes in nature caused by her and Oberon's quarrelling. Sum up the main points/consequences mentioned in her weather report in the table below.

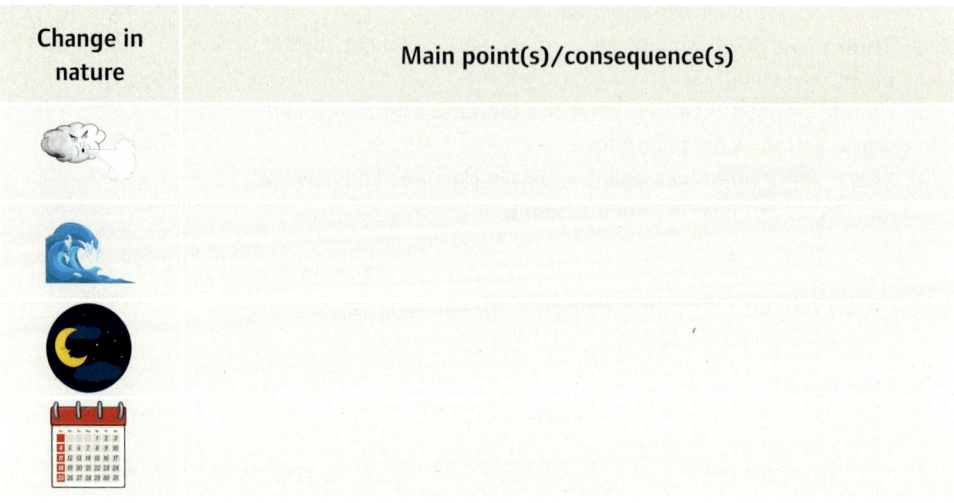

Change in nature	Main point(s)/consequence(s)

3 Read ll. 118–187 of the scene. The action is summed up in statements A–G in the table below. Put them in the correct order by writing numbers 1–7 in the right column.

Statement	Order
A Puck leaves to carry out Oberon's order.	
B Oberon decides to punish his wife for her refusal to grant him his wish.	
C Titania explains her reasons for keeping the changeling boy.	
D Oberon tells Puck about the magic powers of a little flower.	
E Oberon outlines his scheme to trick Titania into doing what he wants.	
F Oberon asks Titania to give up the changeling boy.	
G Titania invites Oberon to join her and her fairies.	

Analysis
4 Examine the dramatic function of the passages dealt with in tasks **2** and **3**.

5 a Read Oberon's speech in ll. 176–187 and try out different ways of speaking it, e.g. sarcastically, angrily or full of glee.

b `Speaking` Decide which attitude fits which part best and perform the speech in a dramatic reading to the class.

Beyond the text

6 a Though the changeling boy is not listed among the characters, many directors have chosen to put him onstage when Titania and Oberon are fighting about him. Create a design for the changeling boy in this scene and draw a sketch of the character.

b Discuss the theatrical function of the changeling boy's role and how the audience's response to the scene could change if he were actually present.

c Speculate on possible reasons why Oberon wants to take the child from Titania.

d If you had to give custody of the boy to either Titania or Oberon, which one would you choose? Discuss with a partner.

7 `Writing` Nowadays, Titania would have reason to accuse mankind of bringing chaos into the natural world. State the most important current manmade environmental issues and their effect on our lives. Write the speech she would give to global leaders to persuade them to take more efficient action.

B6 Fool for love (Act II, Scene 1, ll. 176–268)

`Reading` Read the rest of Scene 1 and complete tasks 1–6.

Comprehension

1 Correct the mistakes in the following sentences.

> **A** Oberon is planning to send a forest animal to attack Titania.
>
> **B** Demetrius regrets that he cannot love Helena in return.
>
> **C** Helena is worried that Demetrius might harm her.
>
> **D** Oberon plans to smear Demetrius' eyes with the love juice.

Who loves whom?
Entering the woods

Hermia	Helena
Lysander	Demetrius

2 Use arrows in the box on the right to show who loves whom when entering the woods.

Analysis

3 a `Viewing` Using the webcode on the right, go online and watch the Royal Shakespeare Company's video 'Exploring a Duologue' from the series *The Text Detectives*.

www.cornelsen.de
code: paduho

b Apply what is said in the video about shared language, questions and answers as well as names and status to your reading of Demetrius' and Helena's duologue (ll. 188–244). Illustrate your findings with several examples.

4 Analyse the imagery used in Oberon's description of Titania's resting place and his plan of action. Point out the effect which is created (ll. 248–258).

Beyond the text

5 a Think: Think about your personal reaction to the way Helena pleads with Demetrius.

b Pair: `Speaking` With a partner, exchange your ideas from **a** and find reasons why she might behave like she does.

c Share: `Speaking` Share your findings with the class. As a class, discuss more realistic ways to help Helena solve her dilemma than Oberon's use of magic.

6 a Create a costume and stage design for the fairy world in the Athenian woods that captures the spirit of the place as described in the text.

b `Speaking` Present your creations in a gallery walk activity. Explain your choice for the fairy costumes and the intended overall effect of your concept on the audience.

B7 Spellbound (Act II, Scene 2)

`Reading` Read Scene 2 and complete tasks 1–7.

Comprehension

1 Divide the dialogue into sense units which match the headings in the table below. Number the headings in the correct order and add the line numbers on the right.

Heading	Order	Line(s)
A Mission accomplished		
B A nightmare come true		
C A little night music		
D Single beds		
E A man transformed		
F A wicked spell		

2 Use arrows in the box on the right to show who loves whom after the first love juice has been applied.

Analysis

3 **a** Analyse the rhythm of Puck's speech in ll. 66–83, comparing it to the metre used by the mortals in this scene.

   b Explain the effect Puck's lines have.

4 Examine the effect the frequent change of pace has in this scene.

5 **a** At the end of this scene, both Helena and Hermia are troubled. Read what they say in ll. 123–134 and ll. 145–156 and compare their sorrows.

   b Discuss which predicament you find worse.

Beyond the text

6 **a** Imagine Puck has several Puck clones with him that are acting as a chorus. Prepare a dramatic reading of the passage with one of you reading Puck and the others echoing key words or making fitting sounds to enhance the overall effect.

   b **Speaking** Present your dramatic reading of the passage to the class.

7 **a** Imagine you were asked to set Titania's lullaby to music for your school's production of the play. Find suitable music and prepare to explain your choice.

   b **Speaking** Present your music to the class.

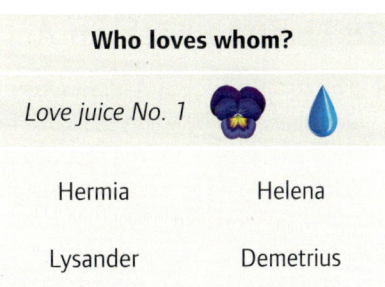

Who loves whom?		
Love juice No. 1	🌸	💧
Hermia		Helena
Lysander		Demetrius

B8 Looking back on Act II

1 The complex plot of *A Midsummer Night's Dream* can be followed and illustrated by using the icons from the key below. Fill in the table on the next page for the first two acts with little icon drawings and continue doing so while working on the rest of the play.

Key:

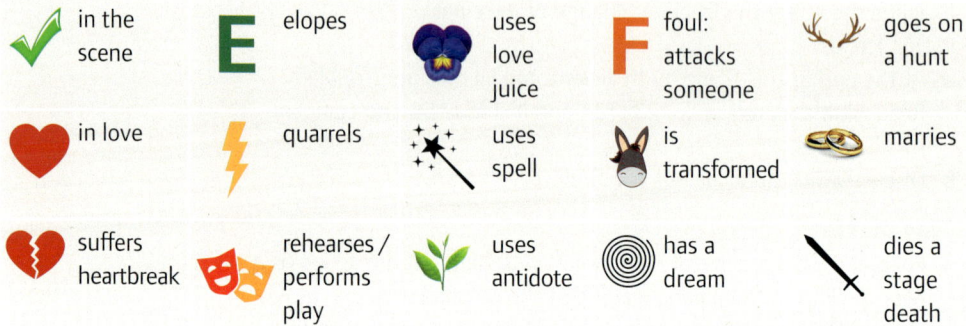

✓ in the scene	E elopes	uses love juice	F foul: attacks someone	goes on a hunt
♥ in love	quarrels	uses spell	is transformed	marries
💔 suffers heartbreak	rehearses / performs play	uses antidote	has a dream	dies a stage death

2 a In four groups, describe the setting, the environment, the characters, the social status and the rules of the four worlds, i.e. the Court, the Lovers, the Mechanicals and the Fairies. Each group looks at one of the four worlds.

  b Create a meme reflecting the spirit of the people of the world your group worked on and design a coat of arms or badge they would want to have.

3 Explain the way both themes of *Men controlling women* as well as *Women defying men* are represented in Acts I and II.

B9 A donkey lover (Act III, Scene 1)

Reading Read Scene 1 and complete tasks 1–7.

Comprehension

1 **Speaking** Imagine a curious neighbour has followed the Mechanicals into the woods, observed their rehearsal and then ran away with the others. In a one-minute talk, summarise what the neighbour would tell their friends about the nightly events (ll. 1–100).

2 **Writing** Imagine a fairy who has watched Puck's prank wants to post the information on his latest mischief on her blog *puck.fandom*. Write her blog entry in which she sums up what happens in ll. 101–177.

	Act I, Scene 1	Act I, Scene 2	Act II, Scene 1	Act II, Scene 2	Act III, Scene 1	Act III, Scene 2	Act IV, Scene 1	Act IV, Scene 2	Act V, Scene 1
Theseus									
Hippolyta									
Philostrate									
Egeus									
Hermia									
Helena									
Lysander									
Demetrius									
Oberon									
Titania									
Puck									
Fairies									
Quince									
Bottom									
Flute									
Snout									
Snug									
Starveling									

Analysis

3 Compare Titania's declaration of love to Bottom in this scene with what Helena says to Demetrius about her feelings for him in Act II, Scene 1, ll. 195–244.

Beyond the text

4 Discuss what the Mechanicals misunderstand about the nature of theatrical illusion.

5 Change plays a big role in this scene. Evaluate the effect Shakespeare achieved with this dramaturgical device.

6 Discuss why Bottom's statement that 'Reason and love keep little company together nowadays' (ll. 122–123) is apt at this point in the play but also true for characters shown in Acts I and II.

7 A member of your school's drama group needs advice: They want to design a donkey's head for their production of A Midsummer Night's Dream, but it cannot hide the actor's face nor be too overdone. Discuss your ideas with a partner.

B10 Overview (Act III, Scene 2, ll. 1–40)

Act III, Scene 2, ll. 1–40

Wondering if his love juice has already worked on Titania, Oberon is delighted to hear from Puck that she is now in love with a 'monster', a man with a donkey's head. His servant also spread the juice on a man wearing Athenian clothes, as he was instructed to do.

B11 Love triangle (Act III, Scene 2, ll. 41–377)

Comprehension

1 a Read the passage which describes the meeting of all four lovers (ll. 41–377). Fill in the table below with a suitable heading for each section. The first one has already been done for you as an example. Don't forget the ones on the next page.

Section	Heading
A ll. 41–87	A serious accusation
B ll. 88–121	
C ll.122–176	

D ll. 177–281

E ll. 282–344

F ll. 345–377

b Use arrows in the box on the right to show who loves whom after the second love juice has been applied.

c Outline each of the four lovers' problems and conflicting aims at this point in the play.

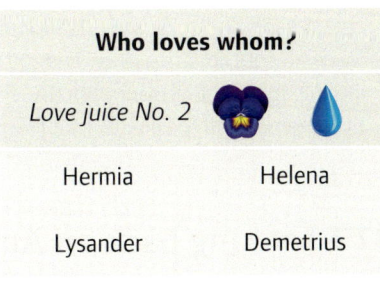

Who loves whom?

Love juice No. 2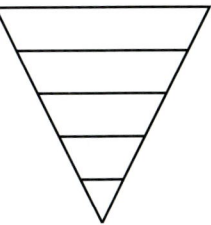

Hermia	Helena
Lysander	Demetrius

Analysis

2 a Compare the language Lysander uses when declaring his love for Helena and when rejecting Hermia.

b Rank the insults Lysander directs at Hermia from least to most hurtful (ll. 258–330). Use an inverted pyramid diagram with the most offensive remark placed at the top.

3 While both Oberon and Puck are onstage and invisible, they observe the lovers' quarrel. Think about ways their presence could be made interesting to the audience. Draw a bird's eye view diagram of all characters' placement and movement throughout the scene.

Beyond the text

4 Discuss who you feel the most sympathy for in this scene.

Language help

deceived/betrayed/cheated · drugged [drʌgd] · mocked/ridiculed · jealous · helpless · regret/feel sorry for · furious · humiliated/scorned [skɔːnd] · disappointed · offended/insulted · feel pity for sb./sth. · rejected/jilted [dʒɪltɪd] · be outraged by sb./sth. · desperate · determined · overwhelmed

---

5 a **Viewing** Using the webcode on the right, go online and listen to the song 'Chasing my Tail' from the 2022 musical *The Lovers*, which illustrates Helena's romantic dilemma. Note down the main points made in the song.

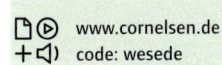

www.cornelsen.de
code: wesede

b **Writing** Write the song lyrics Hermia could sing to describe her experiences in this scene.

6 a Imagine Oberon had to defend his actions in front of an ethics committee that challenges his decisions. Prepare Oberon's justifications and the questions he could be asked about his treatment of Titania and the lovers.

b **Speaking** Stage the interview with one student being Oberon and the rest of the class being his interrogators. Take turns playing Oberon in the hot seat.

B12 Overview (Act III, Scene 2, ll. 278–463)

Act III, Scene 2, ll. 278–463

Puck realises that he must hurry to carry out his orders because dawn is approaching. He spreads fog in the woods to stop Lysander and Demetrius from duelling. Then he leads all four lovers astray. They are all so confused and exhausted that they lie down and sleep on the ground. Finally, Puck squeezes the antidote to the love juice on Lysander's eyes to release him from the magic spell.

B13 Looking back on Act III

1 Use arrows in the box on the right to show who loves whom after the third love juice has been applied.

2 **a** In three big groups, examine how the themes of *Disorder and harmony*, *Gender roles* and *Contrast* are dealt with in Acts I-III. Each group works on one theme.

   b Share your findings with the rest of the class.

3 **a** `Writing` The characters in *A Midsummer Night's Dream* are not fully rounded, but rather stock characters or stereotypes with a particular function. Write mini portraits of all characters.

   b Explain why Shakespeare might have chosen this way of representation.

4 **a** Create an atmospheric soundscape for this enchanted forest with fairy, nature and animal sounds as well as the noises the people who went there make. Think about how the magic spell moment could have a very theatrical effect.

   b Play your audio file to the class.

Who loves whom?

Love juice No. 3 🌿 💧

Hermia   Helena

Lysander   Demetrius

B14 The fierce vexation of a dream (Act IV. Scene 1)

`Reading` Read Scene 1 and complete tasks 1–5.

Comprehension

1 Match the sentence halves on the next page to create correct statements.

1 Bottom enjoys being spoiled by the fairies …	**A** … but doesn't realize that he is under a love spell.
2 Titania is reconciled with Oberon …	**B** … but is overruled by Theseus.
3 Egeus demands Lysander's punishment …	**C** … but they are ready to follow Theseus back to Athens.
4 Demetrius says he loves Helena again …	**D** … but cannot put it into words when he is awake.
5 The lovers are confused about what happened during the night …	**E** …. but has given up the changeling boy while under his spell.

Analysis

2 Examine the means used to highlight Bottom's 'donkeyness' in ll. 1–43.

3 Analyse the dramatic function of this scene.

4 Using a Venn diagram with three circles, compare the reactions of the characters who have woken up: Titania, Bottom and the lovers. The very centre of the diagram contains what all six characters have in common.

Beyond the text

5 Writing Write a new scene in modern English in which Oberon tells Titania how she was found sleeping alongside mortals on the ground. Decide how truthful he is going to be.

B15 Overview (Act IV, Scene 2)

Act IV, Scene 2

The Mechanicals have returned to Athens and are frustrated because they cannot find Bottom, without whom their play cannot be performed. Snug tells them that Theseus and other lords and ladies have gotten married. Suddenly Bottom appears without telling them where he was and announces that their play was 'preferred' for the wedding ceremony. He organizes their preparations quickly and they all leave for the palace.

B16 Looking back on Act IV

1 In order to define the relationships between the characters in *A Midsummer Night's Dream*, match the numbers of the following organigram to the descriptions listed below it. Use the box at the bottom of the page to write your answers.

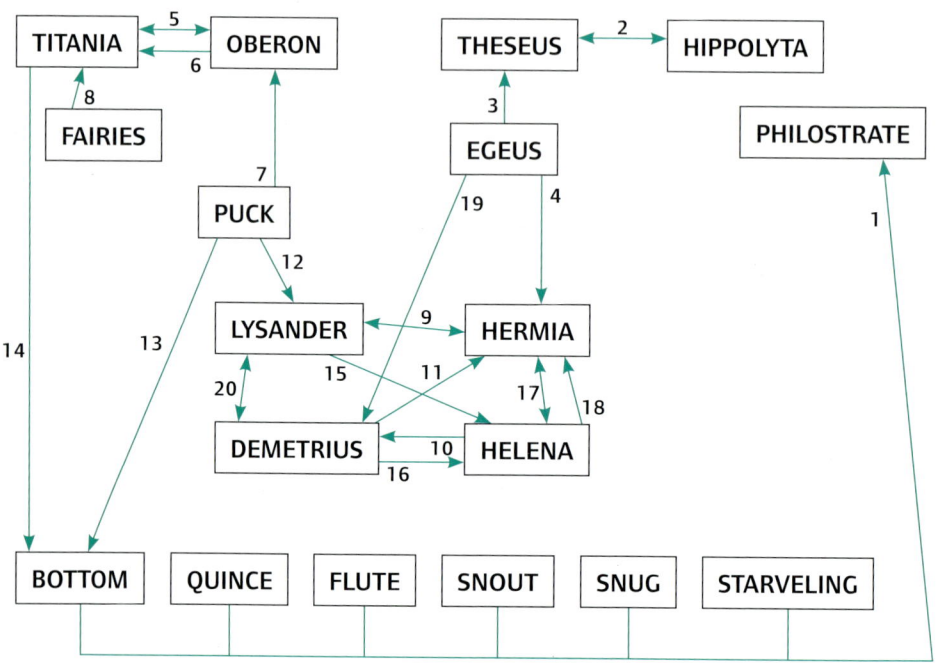

a has the parental support to marry   **b** temporarily loves   **c** serve   **d** asks for help
e remains under the love spell   **f** best friends   **g** serves   **h** transforms into another being
i betrays of trust   **j** father to   **k** engaged   **l** hired by   **m** married   **n** unhappily in love with
o in true love   **p** rivals   **q** prefers   **r** mistakes him for someone else   **s** takes revenge on
t has sex with

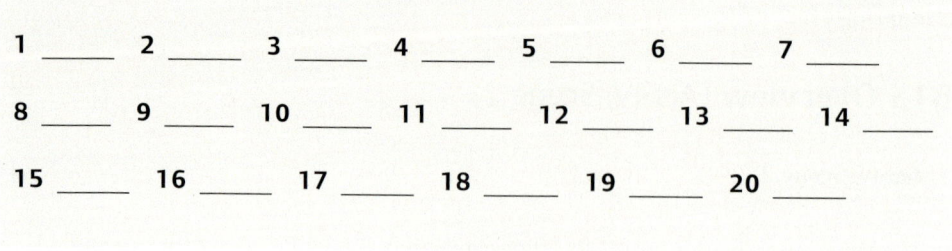

2 Analyse how the theme *Dream, illusion and reality* is treated in Acts II – IV.

3 `Viewing` Watch the segments of the film *A Midsummer Night's Dream* (1999) from 00:23:36–00:30:15 and 00:55:30–00:58:19. Describe the fairy world and the fairies the director has added to the cast. Discuss the effect that is achieved.

4 `Writing` Create an AI chatbot fairy character with an online software such as *Inworld* or *Beta Character AI* and strike up a chat conversation about fairies with it.

5 Refer back to your descriptions of the four worlds (**B8, 2a**, p. 80) and continue working in the same groups to outline the changes each world and its characters have undergone as well as their mutual interaction up to the end of Act IV.

B17 Overview (Act V, Scene 1, ll. 1–105)

Act V, Scene 1, ll. 1–105

In the palace, Theseus and Hippolyta discuss what the lovers have told them about their experiences in the forest. While Hippolyta believes them, Theseus is sceptical because love and imagination can create delusions - especially for people with overactive brains like lovers, poets and madmen. After the lovers have joined them, Theseus asks his Master of the Revels, Philostrate, what entertainment is available and dismisses all offerings but the workman's play which promises 'very tragical mirth' in a 'tedious and brief' show. Despite Philostrate's insistence that the actors are terrible, Theseus orders them to perform because he thinks good intentions matter more than competence.

B18 Send in the clowns (Act V. Scene 1. ll. 106–420)

Comprehension

1 Read the rest of the scene and complete the sentences below. Don't forget the ones on the next page.

A Understanding Quince's first ten lines is difficult because _____

_____.

B In the rest of the prologue, Quince _____.

C Snout (as the Wall) tells his audience that _____.

D Bottom and Flute, separated by the Wall, speak about _____

_____.

E Snug and Starveling enter to explain that _____

_____.

F Theseus and the lovers continuously _____.

G Bottom and Flute, passing as Pyramus and Thisbe, both _____.

H After the court has retired to bed, _____.

Analysis

2 Examine the function and the dramatic impact of the play-within-the-play.

3 Draw a seating and movement sketch map for the performance of *Pyramus and Thisbe* which allows for interaction between the actors and their onstage audience, and ensures that the real theatre audience can see the full cast throughout.

Beyond the text

4 a **Viewing** Watch the performance of *Pyramus and Thisbe* in Hoffman's film (01:33:18–01:46:03).

  b Examine the means the filmmakers used to create comedy and assess whether they have achieved their aim.

  c **Speaking** Stage your own dramatization of Quince's prologue (ll. 126–150) with much comic business for Wall, Lion, Moonshine and the tragic lovers.

5 a **Writing** Write a play review of the Mechanicals' version of *Pyramus and Thisbe* from Philostrate's perspective. Comment on the actors' performances, the text of the play, its scenery and props and include the audience's reaction to the show. Add a rating and a recommendation to your article.

  b Imagine a reporter asks Quince for an interview after the show. With a partner, find suitable questions and replies, e.g. for
    – how Quince thought the play was received,
    – what he thought of his actors' performances,
    – what his plans are for the next play.

  c **Speaking** Practice the dialogue and perform it for the class.

  d Design the poster and programme the Mechanicals could have created for their performance of *Pyramus and Thisbe*. Include the actors' biographies, the parts they are playing, a plot synopsis that does not reveal the ending and a special thanks to Theseus.

B19 Looking back on Act V

1 Examine the function and importance of the forest as opposed to the city of Athens as the place of action for most of the play, including the fairies' visit to the palace at the end.

2 **a** Shakespeare pokes fun at amateur theatre groups. Illustrate the instances of bad acting shown in Act III, Scene 1 and Act V, Scene 1.

b Discuss what you consider to be qualities of good acting.

3 *A Midsummer Night's Dream* contains comedy on several levels. Analyse the comic aspects of characters, action and language.

B20 Looking back at the drama

1 **a** Viewing Using the webcode on the right, go online and watch the TED-Ed video 'Should you care what your parents think?' about the so-called 'Romeo and Juliet effect'.

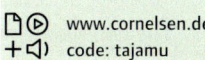

www.cornelsen.de
code: tajamu

b With a partner, discuss the points made in the film.

2 Writing Imagine you want to play a role in your school's English language production of *A Midsummer Night's Dream*. Choose the part you want to audition for and write an email to the director of the play in which you explain your choice and why you think you would be perfect for it.

3 **a** As a class, create a human continuum – form a human line of argument from 'totally agree' to 'totally disagree' – according to your views on Samuel Pepys' review of *A Midsummer Night's Dream*.

> *To the King's Theatre, where we saw* Midsummer's nights Dreame, *which I have never seen before, nor shall ever again, for it is the most insipid ridiculous play that ever I saw in my life. I saw, I confess, some good dancing and some handsome women, which was all my pleasure.*
>
> Samuel Pepys, *Diary*, September 29, 1662

b Comment on your decision and to what extent you agree with Pepys' opinion. Discuss if young people today can still relate to the play.

Part C
Post-reading activities

C1 Themes

1 a Love and marriage are essential themes that are reflected in nearly all relationships of *A Midsummer Night's Dream*. Think of the characters, couples and dramatic elements the themes of love and marriage relate to and write your findings next to the arrowheads in the two diagrams.

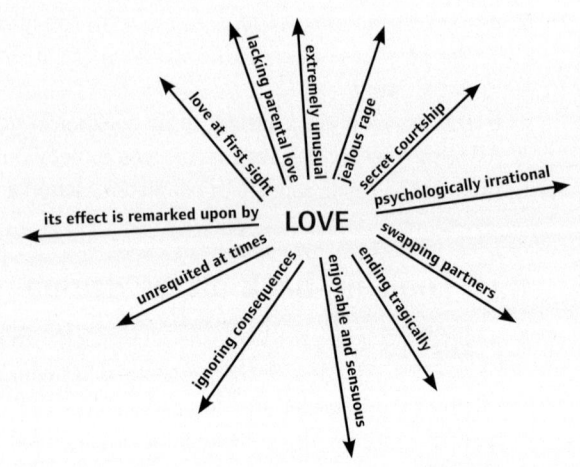

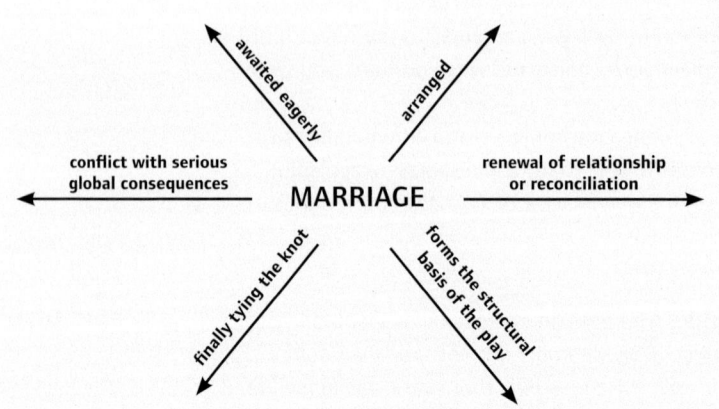

b Explain why Shakespeare might have chosen to present so many aspects of love and marriage in the play.

C2 The structure of the play

Read the info box below and complete task 1 on the next page.

> **Info Dramatic structure**
> Elizabethan playwrights followed classical dramatic theory and divided plays into five distinctive sections. Modern dramas do not follow this structure anymore, but in Shakespeare's plays, it is still relevant in order to understand the pattern of the plot.

The action begins with the **introduction** or **exposition**, which presents the protagonists
and the main plot, and is then driven forward by the **inciting moment**, i.e. an event which
leads to a conflict or problem that needs to be solved during the play. Further conflicts
complicate the plot, and the characters meet more obstacles in the next phase. This is the
rising action. Often, there are sub-plots mirroring the theme or action of the main plot,
which are usually resolved before the ending of the main action. The highest point of
tension is reached with the **climax** or **turning-point**, which marks a complete change for
the protagonist(s). It can either be a change for the better (in a comedy) or for the worse
(in a tragedy). Next comes the **falling action**, which is usually shorter than the rising
action, and contains developments leading to the **resolution** (in a comedy) or the
catastrophe (in a tragedy) that ends the play. In comedies, the characters are reconciled
and marriages are likely, whereas the hero of a tragedy dies.

1 Illustrate where the main elements of drama (bold letters in
 the text above) can be found in *A Midsummer Night's Dream*.
 Which plots would you call sub-plots and what functions do
 the first and the last scenes of the play serve?

C3 *A Midsummer Night's Dream* 3.0

1 **Writing** Imagine a text message conversation between characters
 that is not part of the play, e.g. Puck telling a fairy about his actions
 during the night, Oberon demanding the changeling boy from Titania
 while she is under his magic spell, or Titania arguing with Oberon
 whether it is right not to have given Demetrius the antidote to the
 love juice. Write their conversation.
2 Design a meme or GIF for the whole play and collect your creations
 using an online presentation tool.
3 **Writing** Using an online tool, create a fake social-media profile and
 status for a character of your choice. Write his or her posts and add
 photos, links and video clips they might want to share.
4 **Writing** Write a text which is not part of the comedy, e.g. Lysander's
 love letters to Hermia or the ballad of Bottom's dream.
5 **Writing** Rewrite the narration of a past event in the play in another
 text format, like a song, a poem or a cartoon. You can pick from
 events such as the fairy couple's accusations of adultery, Titania's
 report on the seasons' changes and the changeling boy's mother,
 Oberon's memory of Cupid's actions in Act II, Scene 1 or Helena's
 recollection of her and Hermia's friendship in Act III, Scene 2.
6 Transform the quotes from the play on the next page into emoji
 characters/emoticons and, as a class/group, decide who had the best
 solution.

> Egeus: 'Full of vexation come I, with complaint against my child, my daughter Hermia.' (Act I, Scene 1, ll. 22-23)

> Oberon: 'Wake when some vile thing is near.' (Act II, Scene 2, l. 34)

> Puck: 'Lord, what fools these mortals be!' (Act III, Scene 2, l. 115)

7 **a** **Writing** In small groups, write a newspaper edition covering the events of Act V in different types of articles, e.g. breaking news, a court circular, human interest story, interview, letters to the editor, review or advertisement. Each group chooses a different type of article.

b Once every group is finished with their article, gather them to create a small newspaper entirely devoted to Act V of *A Midsummer Night's Dream*.

8 Create an illustrated one-page response with words and images which expresses how you engaged with either the ideas or themes of the play, a scene, a line or the play's title.

9 **a** Find a brief character description of Orsino and use it to describe the cartoon on the right.

b Imagine characters from *A Midsummer Night's Dream* are using the internet in different ways. Find activities for the prankster Puck, the ham actor Bottom and another character of your choice.

SHAKESPEAREAN CHARACTERS ON THE INTERNET

ORSINO: Carefully curating lovelorn playlists on Spotify

Food of Love
▷ You Belong With Me — Taylor Swift ♡ ⋮
▷ Call Me Maybe — Carly Rae Jepsen ♡ ⋮
▷ Why Don't You Love Me — Beyoncé ♡ ⋮
▷ wish you were gay — Billie Eilish ♡ ⋮
▷ Why Can't This Be Love — Van Halen ♡ ⋮

©2022 Mya Lixian Gosling - goodticklebrain.com

10 a Create a video trailer for a new version of the play. Decide on an angle for the plot (e.g. a fantasy story or a love story), write a narration and choose key scenes without giving away the ending.

b **Speaking** Present your trailer to the class. Explain the stylistic choices you made.

11 a Go online and find modern music for two dances in the play: the fairy couple's dance (Act IV, Scene 1, 83–84) and the Mechanicals' Bergomask (Act V, Scene 1, 337–338).

b **Speaking** Present your music selection to the class and justify your choices.

12 a Examine how Lysander's remark 'The course of true love never did run smooth' (Act I, Scene 1, l. 134) fits each of the play's couples.

b Compare the couples' struggles to the way love is shown in modern romantic comedies.

Info Bergamask
In the play *A Midsummer Night's Dream*, a rustic dance from the Italian region of Bergamo is mentioned: the **bergomask**. Although the spelling with an 'o' is used in the play, it is also commonly written with an 'a': bergamask.

seven methods of killing kylie jenner

Part A
Pre-reading activities

A1 About the author

Info Jasmine Lee-Jones
Jasmine Lee-Jones is a British actor and playwright. She was born in North London in 1998, and was only 21 years old when her first play, *seven methods of killing kylie jenner,* was put on stage in 2019. The play was highly successful and Jasmine Lee-Jones received several awards.

A2 Looking at the form of the play

1 a Make a list of typical features of a dramatic text.
  b Flip through the book. Note down which of the features listed in **a** can be seen. Are there further/new features?

2 a Define the term 'meme' in your own words.

  b From your own experience, list typical features and functions of a meme.

3 a With a partner, flip through the book again and choose one of the memes. Together, imagine a situation in which this meme might be used.

  b Speaking Present your idea to the class.

4 Based on what you have observed in **2** and **3**, make predictions for the play. What do you expect it will be about? Consider the title of the play in your predictions as well.

A3 Looking at the language of the play

1 a With a partner, make a list of acronyms and abbreviations you use in communication on social media.

  b Share your results with the class. As a class, make a list of everyone's acronyms and abbreviations.

2 a Using the webcode on the right, go online and watch a video on how to greet someone in Jamaican Creole (also known as Jamaican Patois) (→ Info box).

  b Do some online research and note down more expressions in Jamaican Creole.

  c Exchange your results in class.

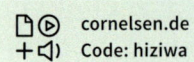

cornelsen.de
Code: hiziwa

Info Jamaican Creole

The two protagonists in *seven methods of killing kylie jenner* are Black British women. Many Black people in the UK have Jamaican or other Caribbean roots because, after World War II, people from former British colonies were encouraged to immigrate to the UK, and a large wave of immigration from the Caribbean ensued. These countries had experienced a long history of colonialization, during which indigenous languages of enslaved African people came into contact with the English of the colonizers. As a result, so-called Creole languages were formed, such as Jamaican Creole (also called **Jamaican Patois**). There are instances of Jamaican Creole in the play, for example:

– 'fi' can be used to mean futurity or obligation, like in #kyliejennerfidead, or to mean 'to', as in 'haffi' = have to.

– 'dem' is the Jamaican form of 'them' and can also be attached to a noun to give it a plural meaning.

– 'blad' stands for 'brother' or anyone who is close to you; just like 'mate' in some parts of the UK.

Part B
While-reading activities

B1 The premeditations

1 a The play begins with an introduction to its historical context in 'Premeditations I', which is said to be optional to the performance. In small groups, research one of the following terms or events mentioned in this section. Make sure each group picks a different topic.

the Corona pandemic (roadmaps and lifting lockdowns)

the Israel and Palestine conflict (around the year 2020)

the #metoo movement

bans on Black hairstyles

hate crimes against Asians

Meghan Markle and Prince Harry's interview with Oprah Winfrey

the Sarah Everard case

the 2020 US presidential election

the US Capitol riots of 6 January, 2021

Breonna Taylor and other female victims of police violence in the USA

conspiracy theories

George Floyd and the Black Lives Matter movement

the removal of statues of former slave owners

b Using the information you gathered in **a**, prepare a two-minute presentation on your topic.

c Speaking Give your presentation to the class.

2 a Read the text 'The Premeditation II' which is the real opening of the play. With a partner, discuss what you think the two women are 'burying' or concealing here.

b Exchange your ideas with your class.

B2 How it starts (Twitterlude 1, IRL)

Comprehension

1 While reading pp. 4–15, answer the following questions:

A What makes Cleo so upset that she starts tweeting about killing Kylie Jenner?

B What is the idea behind the first method (#DEATHBYPOISON)?

Kylie Jenner, reality TV/ social media star, Kim Kardashian's half-sister and owner of a successful cosmetics line, at a premiere in California in 2019.

C What is the idea behind the second method (#DEATHBYSHOOTING)?

D How does Cleo explain her anger to Kara in the IRL-passages?

E What are the first reactions in the Twittersphere like?

Analysis

2 Re-read the two tweets on the first method of killing Kylie Jenner. Explain how they resemble the style of spoken word poetry (→ Info box). Give examples.

> **Info Spoken word poetry**
> 'Spoken word' is a form of poetry that is typically recited orally, for example at poetry slams. Its style is influenced by hip hop, and it often contains word play, different forms of rhyme (end rhyme, internal rhyme), alliteration and repetition.

3 Based on these initial pages of the play, examine what you have learned about the two characters and their relationship to each other?

4 Cleo's Twitter handle (@INCOGNEGRO) is a so-called portmanteau, i.e., a word that is made up of the parts of at least two words that overlap. Explain how the word is formed and what effect it has.

Beyond the text

5 With a partner, discuss whether you consider Cleo's reaction to the Forbes tweet on Kylie Jenner appropriate.

6 Writing Write a tweet in response to Cleo's first tweets (her direct response as well as the first two methods).

B3 How it develops (Twitterlude 2, IRL)

Comprehension

1 Complete the following two sentences by ticking the correct box.

a When reacting to Cleo's tweets in the Twittersphere (pp. 17–20), people …

> **A** feel threatened.
> **B** immediately want to support her.
> **C** make fun of Cleo and show that they do not take her seriously.
> **D** question her moral values, wondering whether this is an appropriate form of social activism.

b In the IRL (pp. 21–27), the main topic of Cleo and Kara's conversation is …

> **A** their friendship.
> **B** Cleo's recent breakup.
> **C** the best form of social activism.
> **D** the difference between Black and white women.

2 After reading pp. 16–27, summarize in your own words what happened in this section of the text.

Analysis

3 Look closely at pp. 16–27. Analyse the different functions of memes in this part of the text (e.g. the memes under 'KARA deeps shit like:' on p. 26[1]). What effect do they have on the reader?

4 Re-read Cleo's monologue on her ex-lover's new lover (p. 26). Make a list of the problematic aspects and analyse what they mean. Fill in the table on the next page to do so.

---

[1]Lee-Jones, Jasmine. *Seven methods of killing Kylie Jenner.* Methuen Drama, 2021, p. 26.

Problematic aspect	Meaning

Beyond the text

5 a When you read the play, you see the memes in context with the words that are spoken. With a partner, collect ideas for the different functions of the memes you have analysed in **3**. How could the memes be integrated into a stage performance? Prepare to perform an example for the class.

b Speaking Perform a short scene with an integrated meme for the class.

6 Writing Write a blog post in which you comment on what the use of the memes you have seen so far in the play *seven methods of killing kylie jenner* says about the influence of social media on the way we communicate.

B4 The fourth method (Twitterlude 3, IRL)

Comprehension

1 While reading pp. 28–40, fill in the gaps below to complete the summary of this passage:

In her fourth method, Cleo proposes to take off Kylie's **(A)** _____

so that she can wear it, thereby taking on Kylie's **(B)** _____ and

(C) _____ for a short time. In the timeline, people are

discussing that they want to **(D)** _____ Cleo, but in reality they

5 are staying because they are **(E)** _____ how the story will

develop. In the IRL passage, Kara tries to make Cleo **(F)** _____ ,

but Cleo turns the argument against Kara by saying that she does not understand the

problem because **(G)** _____ . Cleo lists a number of

examples that prove that **(H)** _____

10 Black women have fewer problems than **(I)** _____ Black women, while

Kara claims that **(J)** _____

share the same problems.

2 Cleo claims that Kara is in a better position because she is lighter-skinned. Kara denies this. In your notebooks, collect the arguments and examples each of the women puts forward.

Analysis

3 Re-read the tweet in which Cleo describes her fourth method. Compare what she calls 'whiteface' with the definition of 'blackface' given below (→ Info box). Where do you see similarities? What are the differences?

> ### Info Blackface
> The term blackface refers to the practice of white actors wearing dark makeup to mimic Black people. It was a regular feature of **Vaudeville shows**, a form of musical theatre that came to the USA through French immigrants and became very popular in the late 19th and early 20th century. Blackface characters often dressed in suits with top hats and performed tap dance. Features of Vaudeville shows were taken over and integrated into US **minstrel shows**, in which Black people were caricatured and ridiculed for entertainment. Today, blackface is considered deeply inappropriate and racist.

4 Refer back to the list of arguments you collected in **2**. Explain how each woman believes she is right. Is it possible that they are both right?

Beyond the text

5 **Writing** Imagine that you are Kara and you have just heard a lecture on the theory of intersectionality (→Info box). Write an email to Cleo in which you explain to her why you disagree with her claim that you have it easier in life. Include all aspects of Kara's personality that you have found out about so far.

Info Intersectionality

The concept of intersectionality describes the way in which the different social identities of a person work together to form their unique position in society. The theory of intersectionality looks at inequality based on race, gender, sexual orientation, socio-economic status, migration status, etc. It assumes that the different aspects always influence each other and cannot be looked at in isolation.

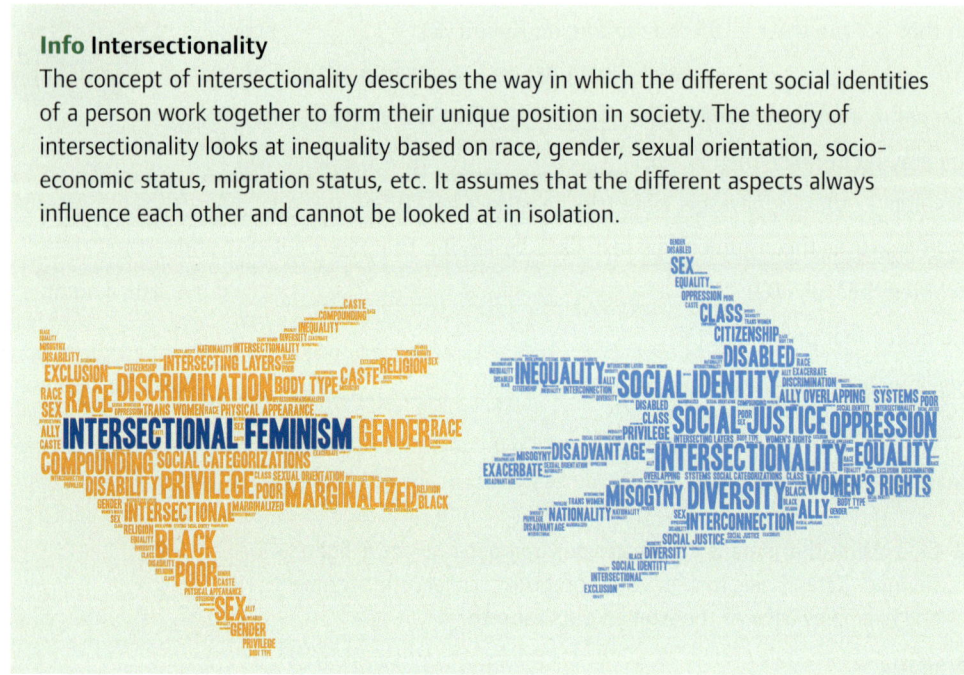

B5 Bringing up old stories (Twitterlude 4–10, IRL in between)

Comprehension

1 Read Twitterlude 4 (pp. 41–42) and fill in the following gaps:

A The fifth method of killing Kylie Jenner consists
of _____.

B The Twitter users compare Cleo to _____ and

post a picture of _____.

2 Read the IRL (pp. 43–49) and summarize in your own words what Cleo says about #wiggate and why it hurt her so much.

3 Read Twitterlude 5 (pp. 50–51) and outline what the twitterlude consists of.

4 Read Twitterlude 6–9 (pp. 54, 56, 58 and 61). Describe what @INCOGNEGRO's critics do.

5 Read the IRL passages following Twitterludes 6–9 (pp. 55, 57, 59–60 and 62–63). State how Cleo defends herself and how Kara corrects her.

6 Read Twitterlude 10 (pp. 64–65) and summarize in 1–2 sentences what Cleo suggests in her 6th method.

_____

_____

_____

Analysis

7 Examine the language of the tweets in the twitterludes. How does it help form a joint opposition to Cleo?

8 a Compare the role of social media in Cleo's past and present. Use the table below.

Social media in Cleo's past	Social media in Cleo's present

b Compare your answers with a partner.

9 In the table below, you will find a list of things,
   taken from Twitterlude 10, that Cleo wants Kylie
   Jenner to experience. Add a sentence of
   explanation for each of the experiences.

Experience	Explanation
'But I want her to [...] The men in top hats Thick full red lips Tap shoes' (p. 64)[1]	
'I want her to have Aamito's lips and Hottentot Venus' hips Without it being called a trend' (p. 64)[2]	
'I want her to be called blick in the playground Drop lip' (p. 64)[3]	
'I want her to be whipped And put in a box on show for a paying audience' (p. 64)[4]	
'I want her to replace her lip kits for cocoa butter or Vaseline' (p. 64)[5]	
'I want her thighs to be called fat not thick' (p. 64)[6]	
'I want her [...] no-lye relaxer and hotcomb [...] her edges to get burnt [...] boxer braids to turn into canerows' (p. 65)[7]	
'I want her to taste the salt tears [...] at 9 When she is told she's not pretty enough for Cinderella' (p. 65)[8]	

[1-8]: Lee-Jones, Jasmine. *Seven methods of killing Kylie Jenner.* Methuen Drama, 2021, p. 64–65.

Beyond the text

10 a In this section, there is a very quick sequence of twitterludes and short IRL passages. Twitter and real life seem to merge. In small groups, discuss how this could be presented on stage. Consider what messages you would want to bring across with the help of stage design. Make drawings to illustrate your ideas.

b Speaking Present your ideas in the form of a gallery walk and discuss your ideas with other groups.

B6 The end of the play (IRL and The post-mortem)

Comprehension

1 Read the final section of the play (pp. 69–83) and answer the following questions by ticking the correct answer.

a Both Kara and Cleo feel that …

- **A** they should both talk about the past.
- **B** they now understand each other better.
- **C** the other should acknowledge her mistakes.
- **D** they should let go of the hurtful events of the past and move on.

b Cleo is hurt because Kara …

- **A** loves her.
- **B** shaved her head.
- **C** told her she was gay.
- **D** officially came out on social media without telling her.

c Kara brings about a change in Cleo by …

- **A** finally apologizing for #wiggate.
- **B** blocking her from her Twitter account.
- **C** telling her why she came out on her timeline.
- **D** writing her own tweets to defend Cleo's tweets.

d In the tweets that follow, Cleo apologizes for her homophobic tweets and says that she …

- **A** was only joking.
- **B** is going to apologize to Kylie Jenner.
- **C** decided not to kill Kylie Jenner after all.
- **D** is going to delete her tweets about Kylie Jenner.

e Cleo admits that, in reality, she ...

    A actually likes Kylie Jenner.
    B knows that she is a violent person.
    C could never imagine killing anyone.
    D has had thoughts about killing Kylie Jenner.

f In the seventh method, Cleo points out that Sarah Baartman ...

    A received a proper funeral.
    B was never known by her real name.
    C was eventually sent home to Africa.
    D received money for being looked at by an audience.

g In The post-mortem, Cleo and Kara ...

    A swear renewed friendship.
    B realize they cannot forgive each other.
    C once again discuss what happened in the past.
    D bury the symbols of what has hurt them long ago.

2 Briefly summarize Cleo's monologue in the post-mortem. How has Sarah Baartman made her feel differently?

3 With a partner, discuss whether your hypothesis from **B1,2a** was correct.

Analysis

4 Examine this passage with respect to its form, the relationship between the Twittersphere and the IRL passage, the characters' language, the use of memes, etc. Consider the message(s) conveyed by these stylistic choices and how this can be applied to your own life.

5 Cleo's monologue (p. 81–82) can be read like a poem. Analyse how Cleo uses rhetorical devices (simile, metaphor, hyperbole, alliteration, parallelism, etc.) to bring her message across.

Beyond the text

6 a With a partner, turn Cleo's final monologue into a dialogue between Sarah Baartman and Cleo in which Sarah asks Cleo questions and Cleo gives answers based on what was originally said in the monologue. Be prepared to present the dialogue to the class.

   b Speaking Perform your dialogue for the class.

Part C
Post-reading activities

C1 Me and white supremacy *Layla F. Saad*

Read the following excerpts from Layla F. Saad's book *Me and White Supremacy: How to Recognise Your Privilege, Combat Racism and Change the World* and complete the tasks that follow on pp. 106–107.

What is anti-blackness against women?

At the end of 2018, Academy, Emmy and Tony Award-winning actress Viola Davis stepped on stage at the Hollywood Reporter's Women in Entertainment breakfast to accept the Sherry Lansing Leadership
5 Award. During her powerful eleven-minute speech, Davis spoke passionately about what it feels like to be a Black woman in Hollywood:

> 'When I started my production company with my husband … we started it because I got tired of always celebrating movies that didn't have me in it … I don't mean me Viola, I mean me as a Black
> 10 woman … I was tired of seeing the expansive imagination of writers when they wrote the mess, the joy, the beauty, the femininity of white characters. And maybe an hour into the movie, you saw the obligatory Black character just kind of walking into the camera, who had a name – didn't really have to have a name –
> 15 because you know nothing about them. And even when you know something about them, it's always so romanticized. We have to be maternal. We have to be the savior. We have to make that white character feel better.'

Malcom X famously called Black women the most disrespected,
20 unprotected, and neglected people in America. I believe that attitude toward Black women applies outside America too. Black women bring up all kinds of feelings in people with white privilege and non-Black People of Color: fear, awe, envy, disdain, anger, desire, confusion, pity, jealousy, superiority, and more. Black women are either superhumanized
25 and put on pedestals as queens or the strong Black woman, or they are dehumanized and seen as unworthy of the same care and attention as white women. Both superhumanizing and dehumanizing are harmful because, as Davis rightly points out in her speech, they fail to capture Black women in the mess, joy, beauty, and femininity of women of
30 other races.

Black women are so often underrepresented because they are not seen as women, let alone as people, the same way white women are. Black women are often painted with a broad, monolithic brushstroke that categorizes them into particular stereotypes that rob them of their

00 supremacy: position of having greater power than sb. else
33 monolithic: (here) massive, imposing, hard to change

105

35 humanity. In the United States in particular, these stereotypes have
arisen out of America's violent slaving history with Black people and
Black women in particular. [...]

As Black women, we even have our own class of misogyny directed at
us: misogynoir. A term coined by African American feminist scholar,
40 writer and activist Moya Bailey, misogynoir is defined as "the particular
brand of hatred directed at Black women in American visual and popular
culture." It is a term that describes the place where anti-Black racism
and sexism meet, resulting in Black women facing oppression and
marginalization under two systems of oppression – white supremacy
45 and patriarchy. Misogynoir reflects the work that law professor, civil
rights advocate, and pioneering scholar of critical race theory Kimberlé
Crenshaw has led on intersectionality.

How does anti-blackness against black women show up?
Examples of anti-Blackness against women include:
50 – The derogatory and one-dimensional stereotyping of Black women
into categories such as strong, angry, servile, sassy, and so on.
[...]
– The underrepresentation of Black women in mainstream media as
the protagonist.
55 – The disdain and disregard toward Black women's style and beauty
in the past, which has now been replaced by the appropriation of
Black women's style and beauty as desirable – as long as they are
placed on bodies that are not Black. [...]

What is anti-blackness against men?
60 [...] When Black men's sexuality is not feared, it is often fetishized.
Black men are often seen as sexual conquests, there to satisfy the white
appetite with their allegedly exaggerated genitalia. They are also
sometimes seen as a means to an end – a way to produce biracial babies,
a way to feel Black (read: edgier, cooler), or a way to anger white parents
65 who would balk at the thought of their white child being in an intimate
relationship with a Black man. [...]

> *From:* Saad, Layla F., *Me and White Supremacy: How to Recognise Your Privilege,*
> *Combat Racism and Change the World,* Sourcebooks, 2020.

39 misogyny: hatred
directed at women
45 marginalization:
process or result of
making sb. be/feel
powerless or less
important

Comprehension

1 Summarize the main arguments of the text.

_____

_____

_____

Analysis

2 Compare Layla F. Saad's text with the play *seven methods of killing kylie jenner*. Can some of Saad's arguments be supported by examples from the play?

Beyond the text

3 `Writing` Write a review of the play *seven methods of killing kylie jenner* (→ Info box) in which you comment on the way issues of anti-blackness are addressed. Refer to Layla F. Saad's text 'Me and white supremacy' in your review.

> **Info Writing a text review**
> Just like in a **film review**, in a text review, you provide information on a text you have read and express your opinion about it.
> To prepare the review, make notes on interesting, positive or negative aspects you notice while reading the text. Find suitable aspects to analyse, e.g. the beginning of the story, the plot development, the characters, the setting, the ending, etc. Take note of chapters or sections in which characters struggle to form their identity. Then structure your ideas. In the introduction of your review, give some basic information on the text and its central theme(s). In the main part, briefly summarize the text's plot and comment on relevant aspects. Finally, give your opinion in the conclusion. State whether you recommend the text, potentially also recommending it for a specific target group. Write from a first-person perspective and use an appropriate register.

4 a In groups, collect ideas on which messages the play brings across with respect to these three topics: ethnic identity, gender and the Twittersphere. How are the topics linked in the play?

b Create a poster visualizing these topics and their interconnectedness. Find or create visuals to add to your posters.

c `Speaking` In a short presentation, present your posters to the class.

d As a class, discuss how this play can contribute to raising awareness of the problems of anti-blackness, discrimination and racism. Include arguments from Layla F. Saad's text in your discussion.

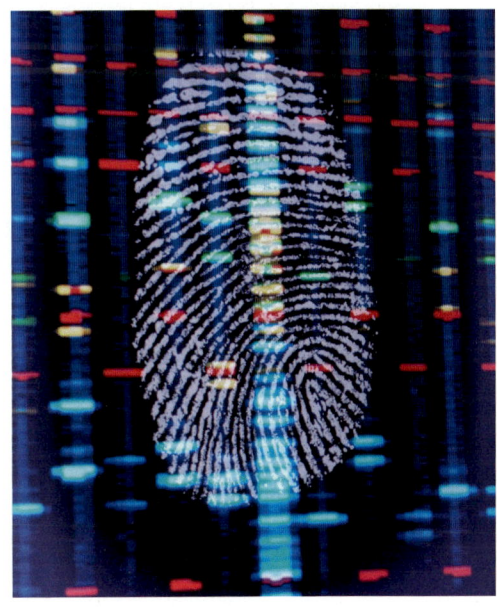

Behold the Dreamers

Part A
Pre-reading activities

A1 Working with illustrations

1 Work on either **a** or **b**.
  a Look at the illustration above. What might it tell you about this module? **OR**
  b Do some research on the different covers of *Behold the Dreamers*. With a partner, discuss what they might tell you about the novel.

A2 Working with the title

1 a Working individually, complete the sentence below:

> A dreamer is a person who …

Language help

aspiration/aspirational · ambition/ambitious · awake to sth. · (be in) denial · illusion/illusionary · innovation/innovative [ˈɪnəveɪtɪv] · nightmare · pioneer/pioneering · fantasize · turn a blind eye to sth. · yearn for sth.

---

b Compare results with your partner. Together, make a table containing positive and negative aspects of being a dreamer.

'Dreamer'	
Positive aspects	**Negative aspects**

c Present your ideas in class.

d The title of the novel contains the imperative *behold*. Use a dictionary to find out what it means, then point out how it might be related to your ideas about the content of the novel (cf. task **1**). Also consider who the imperative might be addressed to.

Info Imbolo Mbue

Imbolo Mbue (born 1981) is a writer of novels and short stories. She grew up in Limbe, Cameroon, and moved to the United States in 1998 to study at Rutgers and Columbia University. Eventually, she settled in New York City.
She gained acclaim for her debut novel *Behold the Dreamers*, which was published in 2016 and won the 2017 PEN/Faulkner Award for Fiction. In her second novel, *How Beautiful We Were* (2021), a fictional African village fights against exploitation by a US oil company.
Her work explores themes of immigration, the American Dream, and human relationships.

Part B
While-reading activities

Use the code below to download a ruler that will help you count the lines in the original text.

B1 From farmer to chauffeur (Chapters 1–3)

cornelsen.de
Code: zevumu

Comprehension

1 Read chapters 1–3 and create a timeline in which you record the most important stages of Jende's career and the Jonga family's immigration process to this point.

farmer in Limbe

Analysis

2 **a** Explain which aspects Clark Edwards considers important in a chauffeur, based on the questions he asks Jende and what he demands from him.

   b Talk to a partner about what a functional relationship between chauffeur and passenger should look like and what both sides should be able to contribute.

3 Examine the atmosphere at Lehman Brothers and Jende's emotional state (Chapter 1). Use the Info box below for orientation.

Info Atmosphere

Atmosphere is the overall mood, the emotional tone of a work of fiction. It is influenced e.g. by elements such as the setting (1), the depiction of characters (2), and the language used (3).

1) Setting is the background against which an action takes place. This includes:
- the location, the scenery, the weather and important objects
- the time (historical time, time of day, season) and
- the general situation (such as the living conditions) of the characters.

2) The depiction of the **characters** adds to the atmosphere. Background information provided about them, the way they behave, speak and/or interact with each other have an effect on the reader.

3) Language-related elements such as the choice of words and stylistic devices such as e.g. metaphor, contrast, hyperbole, alliteration, or parallelism have an impact on the atmosphere.

Many of these elements will also reveal something about the emotional and intellectual situation of the narrator (their 'mood'); however, *atmosphere* is meant to describe the impact on the reader.

Beyond the text

4 Writing Work on either **a** or **b**.

  a After his conversation with Jende, Clark has a chat with his assistant Leah. Write a dialogue in which Clark's reasons for hiring Jende become clear. **OR**

  b Jende is lying in bed thinking about the day. Write an inner monologue in which he assesses how he has performed in the job interview.

B2 Driving Mr Edwards (Chapters 4–13)

Comprehension

1 Read chapters 4–13. The table below contains short statements about them. Write the correct chapter number in the third column. Six of the statements are wrong. Correct them.

	Summary	Chapter	Correction
A	Neni prepares for a maths test at night. It becomes clear that she is determined to achieve good results and to make friends with her classmates.		
B	Jende's brother asks for help since he cannot afford to send his kids to school. Cindy gives Jende a 500$ check to help out, but Jende only sends 300$ because he needs money for Liomi's private French classes. Jende learns that Cindy is afraid that Clark is being unfaithful.		
C	Neni realises that she is pregnant. After a parent-teacher conference, Neni gives Liomi a lecture on how education is the basis for a better life.		
D	Neni asks Jende about his first day at work and the two make plans for their future in the USA. They dream of having their own house with a garden.		

	Summary	Chapter	Correction
E	Jende meets Clark's assistant Leah. Leah thinks Clark is a decent boss but believes that Lehman Brothers and Clark in particular will get into serious trouble.		
F	Jende is informed by his lawyer Bubakar that his asylum application has not been approved. A court will make the final decision on whether Jende can stay in the USA. Jende and Neni stay hopeful.		
G	Jende begins to gain insights into the Edwards's family life: Clark has little time for the family because of his demanding job and the older son is distancing himself more and more from the family.		
H	Jende's lawyer Bubakar gives Jende hope that he will have a very good chance of finally being granted a green card and advises him to keep as low a profile as possible for the time being.		
I	Neni meets up with her precalculus professor to improve her grades but doesn't tell Jende. Her friend Fatou draws attention to the problem of their secret meetings and suspects that her friend is attracted to the teacher.		
J	Jende and Clark talk about Jende's reasons for coming to the USA. Jende emphasizes that political conflicts particularly contributed to his decision. The first signs of a crisis at Lehman Brothers emerge.		

2 Create a family tree of the Jonga and Edwards family and add to it as you continue reading.

Analysis

3 Examine Jende's view of Limbe.

Beyond the text

4 Talking on the phone, Clark mentions 'Repo 105' (p. 40, l. 28), a financial strategy employed by Lehman Brothers (→ Info box).

The Lehman Brothers headquarters in New York, 2008

> **Info Lehman Brothers**
> Lehman Brothers was a large US bank doing business in invest-ment banking, trading, private banking and other services. Founded in 1850, it had become the fourth-largest investment bank in the United States by 2008 with about 25,000 employees worldwide. Its collapse in 2008, caused primarily by its 'Repo 105' strategy (cf. task **b**), was one of the major triggers of the financial crisis of 2007–2008.

a The words in the box below can be used to fill the gaps in the text in **b**, which explains 'Repo 105'. Write down what the words mean.

> subprime loan   cook the books   stock market   debt level
> board member   mortgage ['mɔː(r)gɪdʒ]

b Use the words from **a** to fill the gaps in the text below, adjusting their grammatical form if necessary.

> **Repo 105** was a strategy used by Lehman Brothers before it collapsed in 2008. They
>
> **(A)** _____ as follows: Lehman Brothers concealed the **(B)** _____
>
> that they had given to people with low incomes and poor credit histories. So they
>
> temporarily moved around $50 billion in **(C)** _____ off their books just
>
> before reporting their financial status at the end of each quarter. This made their finan-
>
> cial situation seem better than it actually was because it made their **(D)** _____
>
> look lower. When Lehman's methods were exposed, the resulting crisis hit the
>
> **(E)** _____ very hard. Lehman **(F)** _____ were scrutinized for
>
> their involvement in approving such transactions.

5 To analyse the phenomenon of migration, the social sciences distinguish between push and pull factors (→ Info box).

> **Info Push and pull factors for migration**
> Push factors are the reasons that drive individuals to leave their home country. Pull factors are the favourable conditions of a country that entice people to try to move there.

a Work in groups of 3–4 students. Find current examples from all over the world for one of the categories below. Consider push as well as pull factors.

> **Categories of push and pull factors for migration**
>
> environmental   economic   demographic
>   social   political

b **Speaking** Present your examples to the class and explain one factor in detail (e.g. political factor: war in the Middle East).
c Explain Jende's reasons for leaving Cameroon (cf. chapter 6) assigning them to the categories above.

6 a Referring to chapter 3 (p. 21, l. 1 – p. 25, l. 13) and 6 (p. 71, l. 13 – p. 74, l. 39) point out how Jende is planning to seek asylum.
b Go to the website of the *American Immigration Council* and find out what reasons justify the granting of asylum. Evaluate how likely it is that the judge will grant Jende asylum.

7 a In class, collect aspects about Cameroon that you'd like to present in a podcast. Include the aspects Jende mentions. Assign one aspect to a group of 3–4 students.
b Work in your group, do research and prepare your podcast. Make sure to include local voices expressing their view about their country.

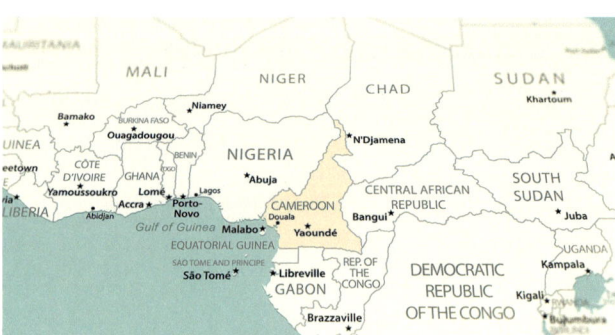

B3 Cracks in the facade (Chapters 14–25)

Comprehension

1 Read chapters 14–25, then identify the correct ending to the sentence starters below. Only one answer is correct. In the right column, add page and line references and a quote supporting your choice.

a At Winstons's birthday party, Neni realizes that …
   A Winston is striving to marry a white woman.
   B Jende is drinking too much alcohol.
   C she feels uncomfortable among white people.
   page + line:
   quote:

b Tom is angry with Clark because Clark …
   A suggests admitting in public that Lehman is in trouble.
   B spoke to superiors about a change of course.
   C prevented selling the company to the Chinese.
   page + line:
   quote:

c Vince tells Jende that …
   A life in the US centres around material success.
   B he is going to India for vacation.
   C his parents are living a happy life.
   page + line:
   quote:

d Back in Cameroon, Neni's father …
   A was a rich merchant.
   B worked for the government.
   C was a respected man all his life.
   page + line:
   quote:

e Cindy …
   A doesn't really care about her sons.
   B is a self-confident woman.
   C is full of fear of being excluded.
   page + line:
   quote:

f Cindy gives Neni her old clothes and Mighty's old toys because she …
   A wants to stop herself talking about her past.
   B fears that Neni could reveal her substance abuse.
   C forgot to give them to charity.
   page + line:
   quote:

g Jende is angry with Neni because she …
   A is not as optimistic about staying in the USA as he is.
   B spends too much time on the phone gossiping with her friends.
   C talks about their problems in front of Liomi.
   page + line:
   quote:

h Cindy has a nervous breakdown because …   page + line:
  A Vince leaves the Hamptons early.   quote:
  B she feels she is being treated unfairly by the people around her.
  C Clark refuses to see a therapist.

i Becky says she would feel bad if she …   page + line:
  A ever took drugs.   quote:
  B found out she wasn't all Black.
  C wore a white woman's clothes.

j Clark …   page + line:
  A is worried that he might not love Vince enough.   quote:
  B shows signs of agreement with Vince's decision.
  C still cannot understand why Vince rejects his way of living.

k Neni doesn't want to tell Clark about Cindy's drinking because …   page + line:
  A he won't take her seriously.   quote:
  B she doesn't want to interfere with their private matters.
  C she thinks Clark knows about this.

l Neni and Jende don't want Mighty to come along to their farewell   page + line:
dinner because …   quote:
  A this would undermine Cindy's desire for security.
  B Cindy has arranged for him to see a friend.
  C the journey to Harlem is too long for just one hour.

Info Patrice Lumumba (cf. p. 103, l. 13)
Congolese politician and independence leader Patrice Lumumba (1925–1961) was the first prime minister of the Democratic Republic of the Congo (June–September 1960). In a political crisis, Lumumba was forced out of office and eventually assassinated. The US government had always condemned Lumumba's socialist ideas as communist views. It is believed to have willingly accepted, if not ordered the killing of Lumumba.

Analysis
2 a Work in small groups and examine the development of Neni's and Cindy's relationship and Neni's status in the Edwards family (chapters 18, 19, 21 and 24). Create a flowchart with the main aspects.
  b Speaking Present your flowchart in class and add aspects if necessary.

3 a Explain Neni's statement: 'That was what made New York so wonderful: It had a world for everyone' (p. 95, l. 11).
  b Comment on Neni's statement, also taking your findings from **2a** into consideration.

Beyond the text

4 In order to describe different forms of integration of people into multicultural societies, three concepts have been developed (cf. the pictures on the right).

  a In the table below, match the definitions given to the concepts by writing their names in the first line of the table.

Pizza

This concept suggests that members from different cultures blend together into a new homogeneous culture, losing their distinctiveness.	According to this concept, different cultures coexist. They maintain their distinct identities, each of them contributing to the whole.	This concept implies that different cultures coexist, but they live in separate communities as parts of the larger community.

Melting pot

Salad bowl

  b With a partner, collect advantages and shortcomings of each concept. Give examples.
5 Evaluate the Jonga family's degree of integration into US society.
6 `Speaking` Work on either **a** or **b**.
  a Imagine you are the US president. Give a speech on the US as a multicultural society. Refer to the concepts from **4** and to what you have learned in class so far. Explain which concept is most likely to be successful. **OR**
  b In your bilingual politics class you are dealing with the three concepts of multiculturalism presented in task **4**. Prepare and give a presentation discussing which type of multicultural society is presented in *Behold the Dreamers*.

B4 Descent (Chapters 26–37)

1 The text below describes the collapse of Lehman Brothers.
Look up the underlined words and explain them.

> Lehman Brothers collapsed in 2008 due to their heavy investments in risky <u>mortgage-backed securities</u> tied to subprime loans. These loans became worthless as housing prices declined and borrowers <u>defaulted</u>. The firm's high levels of borrowing, combined with these massive losses, led to a lack of confidence from investors, resulting in Lehman's <u>bankruptcy filing</u> and sparking a global financial crisis.
> (→ cf. the info box on Lehman Brothers on p. 113)

Comprehension

2 Read chapters 26–37 and answer the questions below.
  a What are Jende's plans for Neni as the pregnancy progresses?
  b Why does Jende fear for his job after the fall of Lehman Brothers?
  c What does Cindy ask of Jende and why?
  d Why is the public so outraged by the incidents at the Chelsea Hotel?
  e What does the reader learn about Jende's asylum application?
3 Describe …
  a the consequences of the fall of Lehman Brothers for Clark (p. 176 ff.) and the public (p. 180 ff.).
  b how Jende changes after receiving the letter from Immigration (p. 224, l. 10 ff.).

Analysis

4 The fate of the two families seems increasingly intertwined. Create a network of relationships in which the interdependencies between the families become clear. Use the family trees you created in **B2**, task **2**.
5 Shortly before the collapse of Lehman Brothers, Jende has a dream about the money doublers (p. 167 – p. 169, l. 9).

  a Look up what a money doubler is and explain their tactics.
  b Analyse the parallels between Jende's dream of the money doublers, the fall of Lehman Brothers and the concept of the American Dream.
6 a The box below contains words related to the American Dream. Exchange ideas with a partner on how the terms refer to this concept.

> upward mobility · homeownership · pursuit of happiness ·
> equality · liberty · success through hard work · freedom ·
> wealth · rights · opportunity

b Work in groups and focus on one character. Explain the extent to which your character has achieved the American Dream, or their version of it. Give examples from the text. Also refer to earlier chapters.

	Aspect/Examples	
	+	−
Jende	Upward mobility/wealth: Job as a chauffeur has changed his life because for the first time, he receives a good salary (cf. p. 29, ll. 30–33) …	Equality: He lowers himself every day to fulfil the wishes of others (cf. p. 83, ll. 21–32) …
Neni		
Cindy		
Clark		
Vince		
Winston		

c **Speaking** Each group presents their character to the class. Complete the table.

Beyond the text

7 The poem below is an iconic text on the welcoming of immigrants.
Read the poem and the info box below, then analyse the poem.

> **Info Emma Lazarus and
> 'The New Colossus'**
> Emma Lazarus (1849–1887) was a US-American writer of
> poetry and an activist for immigration to the US. She especially
> helped Jewish refugees to flee from Eastern Europe where they
> had faced antisemitic pogroms.
> She wrote 'The New Colossus' in 1883 to raise money for the
> construction of a pedestal for the Statue of Liberty in New York Harbor. Twenty years
> later the poem was engraved on a bronze plaque, which was then hung up inside the
> Statue of Liberty.

Emma Lazarus: The New Colossus (1883)

Not like the brazen giant of Greek fame,
With conquering limbs astride from land to land;
Here at our sea-washed, sunset gates shall stand
A mighty woman with a torch, whose flame
5 Is the imprisoned lightning, and her name
Mother of Exiles. From her beacon-hand
Glows world-wide welcome; her mild eyes command
The air-bridged harbor that twin cities frame.
'Keep, ancient lands, your storied pomp!' cries she
10 With silent lips. 'Give me your tired, your poor,
Your huddled masses yearning to breathe free,
The wretched refuse of your teeming shore.
Send these, the homeless, tempest-tost to me,
I lift my lamp beside the golden door!'

1 brazen: made of brass,
also: shameless
2 astride: standing with
legs wide apart
6 beacon: guiding or
warning light
9 storied: famous
11 huddled: standing
closely together
12 teeming: full of people
13 tempest-tost: storm-
driven

8 Analyse the cartoon on the right and compare
its message to the poem's message (cf. task **7**).
(→ Info box: Cartoon analysis, p. 121)

Info Cartoon analysis
1) Describe: Give a detailed account of the elements of the cartoon (objects, text, colours, size etc.)
2) Analyse: Examine the elements of the cartoon and explain their function.
3) Interpret: Explain whether the cartoon succeeds in getting its message across convincingly and why.

9 **Speaking** **Jigsaw:** US Immigration Policy through the ages
 a **Home group:** Get together in groups of five and distribute the topics below among yourselves. Then do research about the period you're in charge of.

A Colonial period (1607–1776)	B Nativism (early to mid-19th century)	C Mass migration period (late 19th – early 20th century)

D Post-World War II (1945 to late 20th century)	E Contemporary period (late 20th century to present)

 b **Expert group:** Get together with students from other groups who worked on the same period as you. Exchange ideas, answer questions and agree on the pieces of information you want to present.
 c **Home group:** Present your results from **b** to the members of your home group. Listen to the other students' presentations and make notes on their findings.

10 **Speaking** Conduct a discussion or debate using the knowledge you have gained in previous tasks. Take the following statement as a basis for discussion:

> Now that the hard work of colonizing a wild land is done, the US is no longer different from the countries from which it first vehemently differentiated itself and no longer has any outstanding dreams to offer.

11 **Writing** Write your own version of (a part of) Emma Lazarus' poem in which you comment on current issues regarding immigration.

B5 The fall from grace (Chapters 38–46)

Comprehension

1 Read chapter 38. List four phases of the encounter between Clark and Jende.

2 a Read chapters 38–46, then fill in the gaps of the following events or ideas from these chapters. The events/ideas are not in chronological order.

A Neni surprises Cindy with a gift at the Edwards's apartment building and eventually confronts her with a compromising photo that prompts a tense exchange, leading to Neni leaving with _____ in exchange for _____ .

B Jende secures two positions washing dishes, but even though he works long hours for six days each week, the combined earnings are _____ of what he used to make at his job with Clark.

C The night after Cindy's funeral, Jende assures Neni that

_____ .

D When Jende gets home, Neni wants to tell him that sharing joy with others when you're sad is _____ .

E Five weeks after Neni's blackmail, Cindy dies in her apartment due to _____ , and her death deeply affects those around her.

F Realizing that her grocery budget has now shrunk considerably, Neni reminisces about _____ .

G Jende is upset with Neni and tells her that he wants nothing to do with her _____ act.

H When Jende is in Clark's office, Clark praises

_____ , but informs him that he is fired.

I Neni informs the pastor of her new plan to avoid their deportation, involving her temporarily divorcing Jende and

_____ .

b Put the sentences from **a** in a chronological order. Enter the letter of each sentence in the table below.

38	39	40	41	42	43	44	45	46

Analysis

3 a Make sure you know what the adjectives in the box below mean, then classify them as either positive or negative by marking them in different colours.

> adaptive · ambitious · caring · compassionate · courageous ·
> determined · devoted · empathetic · hardworking · impulsive ·
> loving · naive · optimistic · overbearing [ˌəʊvə(r)berɪŋ] ·
> patient · resilient [rɪˈzɪliənt] · resourceful [rɪˈsɔː(r)sfl] ·
> sacrificial [ˌsækrɪˈfɪʃl] · selfless · strong-willed · stubborn ·
> supportive · tenacious [təˈneɪʃəs]

b Work in groups of six. Each of you reads the excerpt(s) given below for one of the chapters. For each of these excerpts, jot down one key sentence that reveals Neni's state of mind. Explain the sentence briefly and examine what character trait of Neni's prevails in the situation, using words from **a** where appropriate.

Chapter 39
p. 254, l. 17 – p. 255, l. 23

Chapter 41
p. 261, l. 7 – l. 23
p. 265, l. 21 – p. 267, l. 15

Chapter 42
p. 272, l. 16 – p. 273, l. 2

Chapter 43
p. 275, l. 1 – p. 276, l. 16

Chapter 44
p. 282, l. 13 – p. 285, l. 15

Chapter 46
p. 291, ll. 13–32

c Compare Neni's character as described in chapters 38–46 with her character as described in the earlier chapters.

123

Beyond the text

4 a **Speaking** In pairs, discuss the following possible motives for Neni's blackmail. Agree on the two most and the two least convincing ideas.

| anger about class differences | anger about Clark's passivity |

| ambition to succeed | anger about racism | despair |

| family-orientation | retaliation | self-preservation |

b **Writing** Write a messenger chat between Neni and a Cameroonian friend in which she explains her state of mind.

c **Writing** Discuss whether Neni's blackmailing Cindy can be called a 'fall from grace' (→ Info box).

Fresco on an ancient house in Engadine, Switzerland showing Eve offering Adam an apple from the tree of knowledge

Info **The fall from grace**

The concept of a 'fall from grace' has biblical origins and is closely associated with the story of Adam and Eve. According to the Book of Genesis, Adam and Eve were created by God and placed in the Garden of Eden, living in a state of innocence and grace. However, they disobeyed God's command not to eat from the tree of knowledge of good and evil and were consequently expelled from the garden – their 'fall from grace'. This event is closely linked to the idea of 'original sin'.

The term *fall from grace* draws upon this biblical narrative and has been used in literature, philosophy, and everyday language to refer to a person losing their innocence, favour, or virtuous state due to their actions or decisions. It has become a widely recognized and symbolic idea, often applied to various situations and stories beyond its biblical origin.

B6 Hopes lost and hopes restored
(Chapters 47–62)

Comprehension

1 As you read chapters 47–62, work on the tasks below. Don't forget
   to make page and line references.

   A *Chapter 47:* Name three reasons why Dean Flipkins does not nominate Neni for
   a scholarship.

   B *Chapter 48:* Name three problems that Jende must deal with.

   C *Chapter 49/50:* List Jende's and Neni's attitudes towards staying in the USA.

   D *Chapter 51/52:* List Neni's, Jende's and Bubakar's ideas about what actions to
   take next.

   E *Chapter 54:* Say why Jende hits Neni in the living room.

   F *Chapter 56:* Name two pleasurable activities that Neni and Jende do after their request
   for voluntary departure is granted.

   G *Chapter 57:* Point out Jende's plans for his life back in Cameroon.

   H *Chapter 60:* Describe Clark's situation now and his and sons' plans.

   I *Chapter 62:* Describe some impressions from Cameroon as conveyed by the narrator.

Analysis

2 In this part of the novel, Neni and Jende are torn between staying
   in the US and leaving. All of the passages listed in the table below
   contain different ideas and motives:

Set 1	Set 2	Set 3
Chapter 49, p. 307, l. 1 – p. 308, l. 3	*Chapter 50, p. 316, ll. 1–21*	*Chapter 56, p. 350, l. 30 – p. 351, l. 5*
Chapter 49, p. 310, ll. 1–14	*Chapter 52, p. 322, ll. 1–26*	*Chapter 57, p. 357, l. 6 – p. 358, l. 7*
Chapter 50, p. 312, l. 6 – p. 313, l. 8	*Chapter 52, p. 323, l. 29 – p. 324, l. 5*	*Chapter 58, p. 361, l. 7 – p. 362, l. 6*
	Chapter 62, p. 380, ll. 11–16	

a Gather in groups of three or four and read one set of passages. Prepare a table like the one below. For each passage, identify the motive expressed and write it in the correct column. Also add the name of the person who expresses the idea.

Example:

Staying in the US		Leaving for Cameroon
	Chapter 48 p. 303, l. 26 – p. 304, l. 26	financial burden: e.g. medical bills, student tuition, support for parents, food and accommodation, resulting in mental distress and physical pain (Jende)

b Find partners who worked on the other sets of passages and share your results with them. Complete the tables with their ideas.

c Speaking Imagine you were thinking about emigrating to the USA. In pairs, discuss which of the motives would be most relevant for your decision to stay or to leave.

3 Compare the funerals of Cindy (p. 289, l. 1 – p. 291, l. 12) and Pa Jonga (p. 301, l. 28 – p. 303, l. 20).

4 Examine which of the passages of this part are narrated from an *omniscient*, and which ones are narrated from a *personal* point of view. (→ Info box p. 63)

Beyond the text

5 Writing Back in Cameroon, Jende decides to write two personal emails: one to Bubakar and one to Clark. In these emails, he focuses on his experience in New York, the idea of the American Dream and his future.

a With a partner, discuss how the two emails might differ from each other in tone, content and judgement.

b Divide the writing of the two emails between you.

c Compare your emails and in class, explain the differences, giving examples from your emails.

Part C
Post-reading activities

C1 The immigrant experience – ideal and reality

1 Go back to your answers to the tasks in **A1** and **A2**. How would you answer them now that you've read the complete novel?

2 Explain the following legal steps and goals on the Jongas' path to US admission and put them in the correct order.

work permit (EAD)	naturalization by marriage

green card eligibility as a crime victim	green card eligibility through employment

birth in the US: natural born US citizen	visitor's/student visa

3 Do some research on the different categories of eligibility for a green card and find out about *one* of them in detail. Take notes and present your results in class.

4 a Work in groups of three. Each of you study one of the diagrams on this page and the next to get a fuller picture of immigration from (sub-Saharan) Africa to the US. Look up any terms that you do not understand.

   b Describe your diagrams to each other.

   c Collect facts that you find remarkable. Present them in an infographic.

Chart 1: Sub-Saharan African immigrants in the United States, 1980–2019

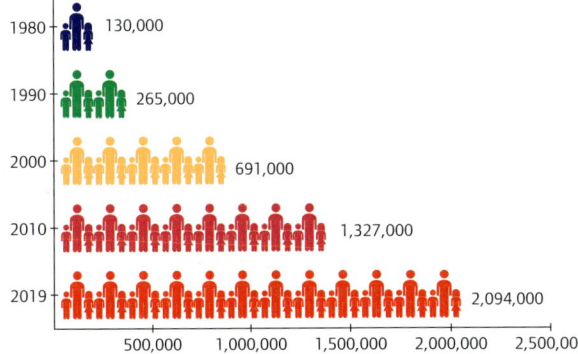

Source: US Census Bureau 2010 + 2019 American Community Surveys (ACS) / Campbell J. Gibson and Kay Jung, Historical Census Statistics on the Foreign-born Population of the United States: 1850–2000 *(Working Paper no. 81, US Census Bureau, Washington, DC)*

127

Chart 2: Immigration pathways of sub-Saharan African immigrants and all lawful permanent residents in the USA, 2020

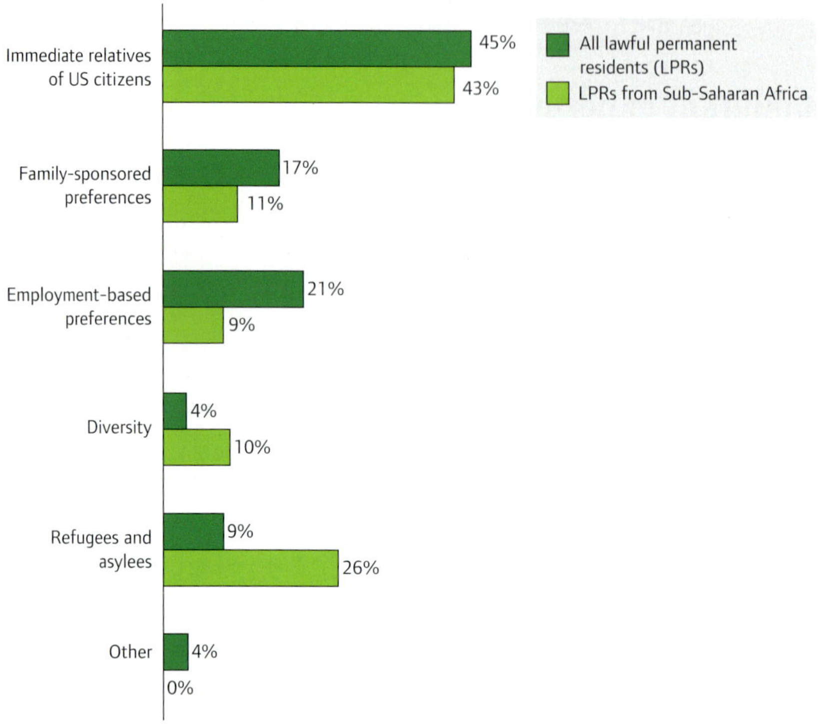

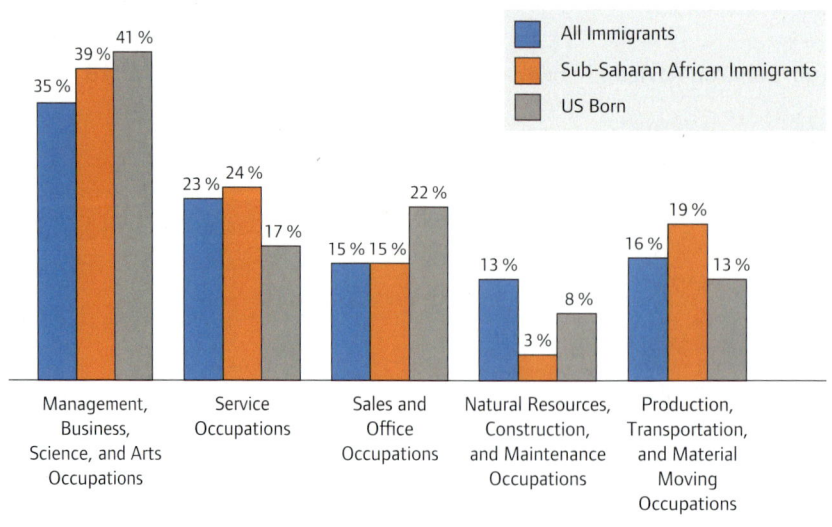

Legend:
- ■ All lawful permanent residents (LPRs)
- ■ LPRs from Sub-Saharan Africa

Immediate relatives of US citizens — 45% / 43%

Family-sponsored preferences — 17% / 11%

Employment-based preferences — 21% / 9%

Diversity — 4% / 10%

Refugees and asylees — 9% / 26%

Other — 4% / 0%

Source: MPI tabulation of data from Department of Homeland Security (DHS), 2020 Yearbook of Immigration Statistics (Washington, DC: DHS Office of Immigration Statistics, 2022).

Chart 3: Employed workers in the US civilian labour force (ages 16 and older) by occupation and origin, 2019

Legend:
- ■ All Immigrants
- ■ Sub-Saharan African Immigrants
- ■ US Born

Management, Business, Science, and Arts Occupations — 35% / 39% / 41%

Service Occupations — 23% / 24% / 17%

Sales and Office Occupations — 15% / 15% / 22%

Natural Resources, Construction, and Maintenance Occupations — 13% / 3% / 8%

Production, Transportation, and Material Moving Occupations — 16% / 19% / 13%

Source: the US Census Bureau, 2019

C2 Questions of African-American identity

1 Do some research on the three celebrities below, their self-image, their perceptions of their Black identity, their stance on racism and their or their family's immigration experiences. Present the results on a poster using e.g. a (Venn) diagram.

Kehinde Wiley, artist
(cf. Module III, p. 43)

Issa Rae, actress, producer and writer

Trevor Noah, comedian

2 Work on either **a, b** or **c**.

a Some sociologists describe US society as 'post-racial'. Why might they have arrived at this judgement? Think about historical events and the situation of African-Americans and other minorities in the USA today. **OR**

b **Speaking** In two groups taking opposite opinions, discuss whether *Behold the Dreamers* is a good choice to treat modern-time racism in the US. **OR**

c **Writing** Write a comment on the state of race relations in the US using the two quotes below from *Behold the Dreamers* as a starting point.

'One of the *[Wall Street] Journal* pages, peeking from beneath sheets of numbers and graphs, had the headline: WHITES' GREAT HOPE? BARACK OBAMA AND THE DREAM OF A COLOR-BLIND AMERICA. Jende leaned forward to read the story, fascinated as he was by the young ambitious senator[.]'

(p. 5, ll. 16–20)

'Liomi sat next to him in the passenger seat, sliding to the floor whenever a police car came in sight. When a white woman pointed out one morning that it was illegal for a child of Liomi's age to sit in the front seat of a car, Jende graciously replied that yes, it was, he knew, thank you so much, madam.'

(p. 126, ll. 1–5)

C3 Cameroon today and tomorrow

1 **Viewing** Use the webcode on the right to watch a video. Create a mind map with information about Cameroon's geography, the challenges it is confronted with, and its future prospects.

www.cornelsen.de
code: widuge

2 **Viewing** Use the webcode on the right to watch a video on Cameroon's president Paul Biya. Tick the right answers.

www.cornelsen.de
code: kidede

1 Which of the following statements about Paul Biya is *not* made in the video?
   A On Monday, he celebrated being the world's oldest head of state.
   B Some Cameroonians are not in the mood to celebrate.
   C Some people consider him to be a violent oppressor.

2 What did people hope for when Paul Biya became President?
   A a state governed by elected representatives
   B less cruelty and bloodshed
   C a strong economy

3 Why did the woman interviewed lose confidence in Biya?
   A Biya's lifestyle
   B censorship of critics
   C imprisonment of dissenters

4 Who challenged President Paul Biya in the 2011 presidential election?
   A Edith Kah Walla
   B Sarah Nwanak
   C Yves Mekongo Mbala

5 What have international observers noted?
   A tension in the English-speaking regions
   B irregularities in the election procedures
   C Biya's long absences from Cameroon

6 Which statement is true about taxi driver Kuam Eve?
   A He criticizes Biya for spending extended periods of time in Europe.
   B He says he can earn a decent income as a taxi driver.
   C He suspects that someone might overhear the interview.

7 What does former minister Elvis Ngolle Ngolle suggest as an advantage of President Biya's advanced age?
   A more authority
   B more tolerance
   C more international cooperation

8 Paul Shooter is a popular journalist and ...
    A a politician of the opposition.
    B a recent victim of violent assault.
    C an activist for the English-speaking regions.

9 Which statement is true about journalists in Cameroon?
    A They fear for their lives.
    B The UN failed to condemn their treatment in Cameroon.
    C Four of them were arrested in the last weeks.

Viewing for gist
10 Which statement fits the general idea of the film best?
    A It aggressively criticizes Biya.
    B It is a neutral report about Biya's accomplishments and failures.
    C It predominantly gives voice to Biya's critics.

Fotos

S. 7/u.r.: Shutterstock.com/Cassi Lee Photos; S. 7/o.: Shutterstock.com/Brian A Jackson; S. 10/o.r.: Depositphotos/Gilmanshin Ruslan; S. 10/m.r.: mauritius images/The History Collection/Alamy; S. 12/u.r.: Shutterstock.com/Michal Chmurski; S. 14/o.: Shutterstock.com/AdriaVidal; S. 15/u.m.: Depositphotos/ani Spooner; S. 19/u.r.: Shutterstock.com/Seita; S. 20/o.r.: mauritius images/Matt Crossick/Alamy/Alamy Stock Photos; S. 21/m.r.: Imago Stock & People GmbH/imago images/Mary Evans; S. 21/u.m.: Shutterstock.com/GoodStudio; S. 22/m.: Galerie Bilderwelt/Bridgeman Images; S. 23/m.: stock.adobe.com/Goldengel; S. 23/u.r.: Imago Stock & People GmbH/imago/United Archives International; S. 24/m.r.: mauritius images/Jim West/imageBROKER; S. 24/o.r.: mauritius images/Historic Images/Alamy/Alamy Stock Photos; S. 26/o.r.: mauritius images/Danita Delimont; S. 28/m.r.: mauritius images/Garden World Images; S. 29/o.r.: mauritius images/Mint Images; S. 31/o.r.: mauritius images/Photo Researchers; S. 33/u.r.: Shutterstock.com/Vlad Kazhan; S. 39/o.r.: stock.adobe.com/Goldengel; S. 40/m.r.: mauritius images/Chromorange; S. 44/o.m.: stock.adobe.com/petert2; S. 45/o.r.: stock.adobe.com/gearstd; S. 46/u.r.: stock.adobe.com/spyrakot; S. 48/u.r.: Shutterstock.com/Madeleine Steinbach; S. 49/m.r.: Shutterstock.com/VH-studio; S. 51/o.r.: Shutterstock.com/Anna Mente; S. 52/u.r.: Shutterstock.com/Hekla; S. 53/m.r.: Shutterstock.com/Margoe Edwards; S. 54/u.r.: Shutterstock.com/Miljan Zivkovic; S. 55/u.r.: Shutterstock.com/fireFX; S. 58/o.r.: Imago Stock & People GmbH/imago/ZUMA Press; S. 63/m.r.: Depositphotos/Oleksii Glushenkov; S. 64/m.r.: Imago Stock & People GmbH/TT; S. 68/u.r.: stock.adobe.com/Georgios Kollidas; S. 68/m.: Shutterstock.com/Mia Stendal; S. 69/m.r.: Shutterstock.com/Lilija Loz; S. 70/m.r.: stock.adobe.com/KHAz; S. 71/o.r.: mauritius images/TopFoto; S. 74/m.r.: Imago Stock & People GmbH/YAY Images; S. 76/u.l.: stock.adobe.com/nikiteev; S. 76/o.l.: dpa Picture-Alliance/Pitopia; S. 76/2. u.l.: mauritius images/alamy stock photo/Patrick Guenette; S. 76/2. o.l.: Shutterstock.com/liu_miu; S. 77/o.r.: Shutterstock.com/shponglerrr; S. 77/m.r.: stock.adobe.com/Eva Almqvist, S&D; S. 78/m.r.: stock.adobe.com/S Curtis; S. 78/m.r.: stock.adobe.com/Fabio Levy; S. 79/o.m.: stock.adobe.com/wacomka; S. 79/o.r.: Shutterstock.com/shiva3d; S. 79/u.m.: Shutterstock.com/ikrolevetc; S. 80/in love: stock.adobe.com/martialred; S. 80/dies a stage: stock.adobe.com/martialred; S. 80/spell: stock.adobe.com/martialred; S. 80/marries: stock.adobe.com/Danilo Rizzuti; S. 80/juice: stock.adobe.com/wacomka; S. 80/transformed: stock.adobe.com/Gstudio; S. 80/u.r.: stock.adobe.com/princhipessa; S. 80/antidote: Depositphotos/Alejandro Sánchez Blanes; S. 80/heartbreak: Shutterstock.com/Martial Red; S. 80/rehearses: Shutterstock.com/MODS; S. 80/n the scene: Shutterstock.com/Arcady; S. 80/has a dream: Shutterstock.com/Martial Red; S. 80/quarrels: Shutterstock.com/Martial Red; S. 80/goes on a hunt: Shutterstock.com/galunga.art; S. 83/o.m.: stock.adobe.com/wacomka; S. 83/o.l.: Shutterstock.com/shiva3d; S. 83/u.r.: Shutterstock.com/Brovko Serhii; S. 84/o.m.: Depositphotos/Alejandro Sánchez Blanes; S. 84/u.: Shutterstock.com/Robert Kneschke; S. 84/u.r.: Shutterstock.com/shiva3d; S. 85/m.r.: -stock.adobe.com/bsd studio; S. 87/o.r.: Shutterstock.com/Anywheredoor; S. 89/o.r.: stock.adobe.com/2ragon; S. 91/m.r.: Shutterstock.com/studiovin; S. 92/m.r.: Good Tickle Brain/Mya Lixian Gosling; S. 93/m.: stock.adobe.com/Urupong; S. 93/u.r.: mauritius images/alamy stock photo/SOPA Images Limited; S. 94/m.r.: Shutterstock.com/wongstock; S. 96/u.r.: stock.adobe.com/Rey; S. 96/o.r.: Imago Stock & People GmbH/Everett Collection/Adrian Cabrero/Everett Collection; S. 98/u.r.: stock.adobe.com/Alexandru; S. 99/o.r.: stock.adobe.com/James Wimberg; S. 100/o.: stock.adobe.com/arloo; S. 100/u.r.: stock.adobe.com/Om.Nom.Nom; S. 100/m.r.: Shutterstock.com/Tom Black Dragon; S. 102/o.m.: stock.adobe.com/kittyfly; S. 102/o.r.: stock.adobe.com/Picture Partners Holland/Picture Partners; S. 103/o.r.: Shutterstock.com/13_Phunkod; S. 107/u.r.: mauritius images/Science Photo Library; S. 108/m.: Depositphotos/Juan Moyano; S. 109/u.r.: Imago Stock & People GmbH/imago images/ZUMA Press; S. 110/m.r.: mauritius images/Peter Titmuss/Alamy/Alamy Stock Photos; S. 110/o.r.: Shutterstock.com/Media Lens King; S. 113/o.r.: Shutterstock.com/udo salters photography; S. 114/u.r.: Depositphotos/Hryhorii Turik; S. 114/u.l.: mauritius images/robertharding; S. 114/o.r.: mauritius images/HemiS. fr; S. 114/m.r.: mauritius images/Universal Images Group North America LLC/Alamy/Alamy Stock Photos; S. 117/o.r.: stock.adobe.com/vladwel; S. 117/u.r.: Depositphotos/Ruslan Nesterenko; S. 117/m.r.: Depositphotos/Olga Dorohova; S. 118/m.r.: Shutterstock.com/rafastockbr; S. 120/u.r.: CartoonStock/Isabella Bannerman; S. 120/o.r.: mauritius images/Science Source; S. 120/m.: mauritius images/Ross Warner/Alamy/Alamy Stock Photos; S. 122/o.r.: Depositphotos/Daniil Zdorov; S. 124/m.r.: Shutterstock.com/Claudio Giovanni Colombo; S. 129/o.l.: Imago Stock & People GmbH/ZUMA Wire; S. 129/o.r.: Imago Stock & People GmbH/Hutchins Photo; S. 129/o.m.: mauritius images/Jeffrey Mayer/Alamy;

Fremdtexte

S. 13: "Über Eheglück entscheidet vor allem die Frau." DER SPIEGEL, 14 Sept. 2014, www.spiegel.de/wissenschaft/mensch/partnerschaft-ueber-eheglueck-entscheidet-vor-allem-die-frau-a-991512.html.; S. 16: "WePresent | the First Feminists: A Story by Bernardine Evaristo." wepresent.wetransfer.com, June 2023, wepresent.wetransfer.com/stories/literally-bernardine-evaristo.; S. 42: Roth, Yvonne. "Gilman, Charlotte [Anna] Perkins" in: Engler, Bernd & Müller, Kurt (EdS.). Metzler Lexikon amerikanischer Autoren. Stuttgart und Weimar: Metzler, 2000; S. 42: Lenz, Susanne. "Nachwort". In. Charlotte Perkins Gilman: The Yellow Wallpaper. Reclam, 1987, pp. 33-48; S. 46: Weldon, Fay. "Weekend". The Penguin Book of Modern Women's Short StorieS. Edited by Susan Hill. Penguin, 1990, pp. 352-371; S. 102: Lee-Jones, Jasmine. Seven methods of killing Kylie Jenner. Methuen Drama, 2021, p. 65; S. 102: Lee-Jones, Jasmine. Seven methods of killing Kylie Jenner. Methuen Drama, 2021, p. 64; S. 105: Saad, Layla. "Me and White Supremacy: How to Recognize Your Privilege, Combat Racism and Change the World", Sourcebooks, 2020, S. 86-90, 93, 95; S. 129 u.l.: Mbue, Imbolo. Behold the DreamerS. Random House, 2017, p. 5; S. 129 u.r.: Mbue, Imbolo. Behold the DreamerS. Random House, 2017, p. 126